Business Administration Reading Lists and Course Outlines

Compiled by James W. Dean, *Columbia University & Simon Fraser University* and Richard Schwindt, *Simon Fraser University*, July 1981

.Vol. 3

International Banking and Finance

eno river press

Box 4900
Duke Station
Durham, NC 27706 USA

NOTE TO USER

These volumes have been compiled and published to serve as an aid in business education. Our intent is to dissem- inate as quickly and as efficiently as possible information on what is being taught, and how it is being taught by scholars and educators in the business programs of leading universities and colleges. We recognize the trade-off between rapid dissemination and polished appearance, and opted for the former. We hope that the users of the volumes will agree with this decision, recognizing that most of the courses represented were given within the last year and forgiving the imperfections which remain uncorrected.

These reading lists and course outlines include both undergraduate and graduate courses. They are intended pri- marily to aid individual professors and curriculum committees in the construction of new courses and the modifica- tion of existing ones. However, we have a less modest goal. Between publication in academic journals and integration into mainstream textbooks, scholarly research passes through the transition stage of classroom exposure. We hope that these volumes will help to speed the transition process.

Depending upon the reception of these volumes by the profession, we plan, from time to time, to reprint updated and expanded editions. We would welcome new or updated teaching materials, especially in emergent or unconven- tional areas.

Acknowledgement

The cover was designed by Robert Steiner, and the volumes were printed by Chapel Hill Printing Company.

Eno River Press
Box 4900, Duke Station
Durham, North Carolina, 27706, U.S.A.

ISBN for this volume 0-88024-015-6
ISBN Eno River Press for the series 0-88024-012-1

Library of Congress Catalog Number 81-69291

Printed in the United States of America

CONTENTS

CONTENTS (continued)

Summer 1981   B8509   International Finance   Professor Michael Adler

A. Outline

The goal of this course is to equip students to deal with some of the major environmental and decision problems relating to corporate overseas finance and investment. Analytical abilities are grounded on the conceptual foundations (some call it theory) developed in the lectures on each topic and via exercises. There will be but one or two cases. Marks will be based on classroom participation, a midterm and a final.

Ideally, a course should make you familiar with the consensus on, or bring you up to the frontier of each of the issues it treats. This may not be possible. Some of you may care to try. I shall be available to those who have such ambitions and, of course, to anyone who feels that I have confused him or her.

The prospective menu of topics for our twelve weeks is:

1. Why do Multinational Firms Exist?
2. Risk and Return in International Finance
3. The International Structure of Returns
4. The Forward Exchange Rates and Forecasting
5. Forecasting Exchange Rates: Other Methods
6. Where Should We Borrow?
7. International Accounting
8. Managing Corporate Exchange Risk
9. U.S. Taxation of Foreign Source Income
10. Decisions Rules for MNC Capital Budgeting

The detailed syllabus follows. The list of readings contains more than the minimum required. I have included, in addition, readings that you may want for future reference. The minimum readings are asterisked (*). I have tried to include in the package only the more inaccessible material.

Note.   Owing to the Memorial Day Holiday, this term is one class-session shorter than the others. To make up for this shortage and to make sure that you get full value, we shall conduct the Midterm examination on the evening of Wednesday, June 24, from 1900 - 2030 hours. Please plan for this.

B. Syllabus

1. 18 May 1981

Why Do Multinational Firms Exist?
Or The Theory of Private Direct
Investment

* (1) Magee, Stephen P.

"Information and the Multinational
Corporation: An Appropriability
Theory of Direct Foreign Investment".
Working Paper 77-11, College of
Business Administration, University of
Texas at Austin, October 1976.

2. 20 May 1981

Risk and Return in International Finance

* (2) Black, Fischer

"The Ins and Outs of Foreign Investment",
Financial Analysts Journal, May-June 1978

* (3) Ragazzi, G.

"Theories of the Determinants of Direct
Foreign Investment," IMF Staff Papers,
July 1973.

3. 27 May 1981

Do MNC's Diversify for Investors?

For those intending to work in merchant banks, the following
references may be of special interest. These include empirical
tests of the basic theory.

(4) Lessard, Donald R.

"World, Country and Industry Relationship
in Equity Returns: Implications for Risk
Reduction through International Diversification", Financial Analysts Journal,
January-February 1976.

* (5) Jacquillat, B. and
        Solnik, B.

"Multinationals Are Poor Tools for
Diversification", Journal of Portfolio
Management, Winter 1978.

* (6) Agmon, T. and
        Lessard, D. R.
        together with,

"Investor, Recognition of Corporate
International Diversification", Journal
Of Finance, September 1977.

Adler, M.

"Comment on Agmon-Lessard", Journal of
Finance, March, 1981

Note: We shall return to applications of asset-pricing models later in
        the course.

4. 1 June 1981

The Forward Exchange Market

* (7) Adler, M.

"International Parity Relations",
(class note, unpublished)

* (8) Adler, M. and
     Dumas, B.
                    "The Forward Exchange Market",
                    (class note, unpublished)

* (9) Kubarych, Roger M.
                    Foreign Exchange Markets in the United
                    States (Federal Reserve Bank of New
                    York, 1978).

  Assignment: Exercises; to be distributed

5. **3 June 1981**
                    Arbitrages and Banker's Swaps

  * (10) Dushek, C. and
       Harding, C.
                    Trading in Foreign Currencies,
                    (American Trans Euro Corp., Chicago,
                    Ill., 1978), pp. 6-22 and 44-52.

  * (11) Adler, M.
                    "Bankers" Swaps, Futures Spreads and
                    the Sensitivity of Bankers' Swap Profits
                    to Variations in the Spot Exchange Rate,"
                    (class note, 1980, unpublished). To be
                    distributed.

Assignment: Determine the sensitivity of spot forward and forward - forward
           swaps to changes in the future spot exchange rate.

6. **8 June 1981**
                    Banks in the Forward Exchange Markets

  * (12) **Case:**
                    City Bank's Foreign Exchange Problems

       Task:
                    Prepare an analysis which fully explains
                    how Citibank generated its loss and
                    evaluate its procedures. A good analysis
                    will utilize actual data from the years in
                    question to reconstruct the possible
                    transactions.
                    Sources: Banking and Quotations, various
                                issues or, IMF International
                                Financial Statistics, various
                                issues.

7. **10 June 1981**
                    Forward Exchange Rates and Forecasting

  * (13) Levich, R.M.
                    "Are Forward Rates Unbiased Predictors
                    of Future Spot Rates?" Working Paper,
                    New York University, April 1977.

    (14) Roll, R. and
       Solnik, B.
                    "A Pure Foreign Exchange Asset Pricing
                    Model:, Journal of International
                    Economics, May 1977. This paper attempts
                    to estimate the risk-premium-bias and
                    gives some idea of the complexity of this
                    task.

8. <u>15 June 1981</u>   <u>Forecasting Exchange Rates: Other Methods</u>

   * (15) Goodman, S. M.   "No Better Than the Toss of Coin",
                                     <u>Euromoney</u>, December 1978, 75-85.

   * (16) Dufey, G. and   "The Random Behavior of Flexible Exchange
           Giddy, I.   Rates", <u>Journal of International Business
                                      Studies,</u> Spring 1975.

   * (17) Adler, M.   Purchasing Power Parity in International
                                      Finance (class note, unpublished).

9. <u>17 June 1981</u>

   * (18) Bilson, J.F.O.   "The Monetary Approach to the Exchange
                                      Rate: Some Empirical Evidence", <u>IMF
                                      Staff Papers,</u> March 1978.

   * (19) Bilson, J.F.O.   "Recent Developments in Monetary Models
                                      of Exchange-Rate Determination", <u>IMF
                                      Staff Papers,</u> June 1979.

Note: For a pragmatic survey of foreign exchange forecasts
       and forecasting services, see "Cover Story", in
       <u>Euromoney,</u> August 1977, pp. 13-41 (not in package).

10. <u>22 June 1981</u>   <u>Guest Speaker, Predex, Inc.</u>

   * (20) Levich, R. M.   "Analyzing the Accuracy of Foreign
                                      Exchange Advisory Services", New York
                                      University, unpublished mss., 1978.

11. <u>24 June 1981</u>   <u>International Accounting</u>

   * (21) Adler, M.   "Accounting for Foreign Transactions
                                      and Operations", B8509 class note,
                                      1980, unpublished.

    (22) Financial Accounting   "Accounting for the Translation of
           Standards Board   Foreign Currency Transactions and
                                      Foreign Currency Financial Statements",
                                      Statement of Financial Standards, No. 8,
                                      Stamford, Connecticut, 1975.

  * Assignment: Exercise on accounting problems
                 (to be distributed)

12. <u>29 June 1981</u>   <u>Managing Corporate Exchange Risk</u>

     * (23) Adler, M. and   "Foreign Exchange Risk Management",
               Dumas, B.   B8509 Class Note, December 1979,
                                          unpublished.

Additional source materials in this area are:

     * (24) Ankrom, R. K.   "Top Level Approach to the Foreign
                                        Exchange Problem," <u>Harvard Business
                                        Review</u>, July-August 1974.

     * (25) Lietaer, B. A.   <u>Financial Management of Foreign Exchange</u>,
                                        Cambridge, Mass.: MIT Press, 1970,
                                        Chapter 2.

       (26) Lietaer, B. A.   "Managing Risks in Foreign Exchange",
                                        <u>Harvard Business Review</u>, March-April 1970.

13. <u>1 July 1981</u>   <u>Should Firms Hedge?</u>

The management of corporate exchange risk is receiving increased
attention these days. While practitioners undoubtedly know what
they are doing, the advice they are getting from theorists is
sometimes conflicting and misleading. The following is an attempt
to provide a conceptual synthesis of the relevant issues.

     * (27) Adler, M. and   "New Issues in Exposure Management"
               Dumas, B.   (class note, Columbia University, unpublished)

       (28) Dumas, B.   "The Theory of the Trading Firm
                                          Revisited", <u>Journal of Finance</u>,
                                          June 1978.

14. <u>13 July 1981</u>   <u>Working Capital Management</u>

     * (29) Donahue, J. C.,   "The Implications of a Hedge",
               Antl, B. and   <u>Euromoney</u>, July 1978.
               Henry, A. C.

     * (30) Donahue, J. C.,   "How to Hedge a Commitment",
               <u>et</u>. <u>al</u>.   <u>Euromoney</u>, August 1978

     * (31) Antl, B. and   "The Hedger Has to Handle a Three-
               Massey, R. J.   Pronged Fork", <u>Euromoney</u>,
                                          January 1979.

There will be a guest speaker today.

Additional technical readings in this area are:

(32) Adler, M.   "Short-Term Multinational Financial
     et al.   Planning", Class Note, unpublished.
                   This is an application of linear
                   programming.

(33) Rutenberg   P.   "Maneuvering Liquid Assets in a
                         Multinational Company: Formulation
                         and Deterministic Solution Procedures",
                         Management Science, Vol. 16, No. 10,
                         June 1970. Assume the solution is
                         found by linear programming rather
                         than by network flow analysis.

Working Capital

(34) Shapiro, A. C. and   "Managing Exchange Risks in a Floating
     Rutenberg, D. P.   World", Financial Management, Summer
                             1976, pp. 48-58.

35) Shapiro, A. C. and   "When to Hedge Against Devaluation",
     Rutenberg, D. P.   Management Science, August 1976. This
                             is a dynamic programming formulation.

15. 15 July 1981   To Hedge or Not to Hedge?

     * (36) Case: Dozier Industries.
                             Prepare a consultant's report to
                             Mr. Rothschild recommending what
                             he should do.

16. 20 July 1981   Guest Speaker: International Portfolio
                                                       Diversification

     * (37) Solnik, B. H.   "Why Not Diversify Internationally Rather
                             than Domestically", Financial Analysts
                             Journal, July-August 1974, pp. 48-54.

     (38) Adler, M. and B.   International Portfolio Choice (class note,
          Dumas   Columbia University, Unpublished)

17. 22 July 1981   Where Should We Borrow or Invest?

     *   Case: Consolidated Industries of Zug

Note: There are basically three methods: (a) invest on a fully covered basis; (b) invest without cover; and (c) invest in several currencies, i.e. diversify your liabilities, with or without partial cover. Try to devise a technique for evaluating each option.

  Addendum: Our coverage of international financial instruments and sources of funds is incomplete. The best source on these topics is Financing Foreign Operations, published and updated by Business International (Geneva and New York). This material, however, cannot be reproduced.

  * (39) Blackie, H. C.   "The Choice of Currencies in Portfolio Management", Euromoney, December 1978, 106-114.

Note: Reading (39) provides little guidance as to the proportions of the risky assets one should choose to include in the portfolio. This, however, is one of the problems in the case.

  You may look for theoretical guidance to reading (38).

18. 27 July 1981   Taxation of Foreign Source Income

  * (40) Adler, M.   "U. S. Taxation of U. S. Multinational Corporations", Class Note, unpublished.

  * (41) Adler, M.   "The Allocation of Interest and R & D Under 1.861-8(e)", The Tax Adviser, October, 1980. To be distributed.

  (42) Ravenscroft, D. R.   "Taxation of Income Arising from Changes in the Value of Foreign Currency", Harvard Law Review, Vol. 82, June 1969, pp. 772-792.

  (43) Eiteman, D. K. and   Multinational Business Finance, (Reading, Mass.: Addison-Wesley Pub. Co.) Chapter 7, pp. 145-187. This is a businessman's guide and is somewhat obsolete.

Additional background readings are:

  (44) Horst, T.   "American Taxation of Multinational Firms", American Economic Review, Vol. 67, No. 3, June 1977.

  (45) Kopits, G. F.   "Intra-Firm Royalties Crossing Frontiers and Transfer-Pricing Behavior", The Economic Journal, December 1976.

19. <u>29 July 1981</u>   <u>Taxation (Continuation)</u>

    * (46) Ashton, R. K.   "Taxation of Corporations in the U.K.".
                                       Class Note, London Business School,
                                       unpublished.

    * (47) Rodriguez, R. M. and   <u>International Financial Management</u>,
              Carter, E. E.   (Engelwood Cliffs, N. J.: Prentice-
                                       Hall, Inc., 1979) Appendix 1 and
                                       exercises.

20. <u>3 August 1981</u>   <u>Taxation (Continuation)</u>

                                       Assignment: Exercise on Taxation.

21. <u>5 August 1981</u>   <u>A Pragmatic Synthesis</u>

    * (48) Brealey, R. A. and   "International Financial Management",
                                   Chapter 32 in <u>Principles of Finance</u>
                                   (New York, N. Y.: McGraw Hill, Inc., 1980)

    * (49) Case: <u>Midwestern Food Corporations (9-271-691)</u>

                                          Assignment: Consider the problems of
                                                   applying the WACOC criterion
                                                   to the MNC.

                                       Note: I am still looking for a good
                                                 reference on MNC capital budgeting.

22. 10 August 1981   <u>Financial Structure for MNC's</u>

    * (50) Case: Tektronix, Inc., case no. 17 in Carlson,
                                   Remmers, et. al., <u>International Finance</u>
                                   (Addison-Wesley, 1980)

23. 12 August 1981   <u>Review and Farewell</u>

COLUMBIA UNIVERSITY
Graduate School of Business

INTERNATIONAL BANKING
(B8358)

Prof. James W. Dean

Summer, 1980

A. Course Content:

This course examines international banking in three contexts:
macroeconomic, regulatory and microeconomic. Thus the course
begins by placing international banking in larger theoretical,
historical and market frameworks. Next the course considers
the currently fluid regulatory environment facing the industry.
Finally, the international bank is studied in its role as a
financial intermediary, taking deposits and making loans.

A term paper is required. There will be occasional guest
speakers.

B. Outline of Topics:

Week		Topic
1,2	1.	Larger Contexts
		Some banking theory:
		Motives for domestic banking
		Restrictions on domestic banking
		Motives for international banking
		Some postwar history:
		U.S. Banks move abroad: Eurodollars
		Non U.S. banks internationalize
		Foreign banks enter the U.S.
		Major international banks today
3		The Eurocurrency: first principals
4		Credit and liquidity creation by international banks
	II.	Issues of Public Policy
5		Eurodollars and national monetary policy
6,7,		Current regulatory issues
8		Foreign banks in the U.S. and the International Banking Act of 1978
	III.	The International Bank as a Financial Intermediary
9		Sources and uses of funds
10,11		Loan practices in international banking
12		Some specialized activities

-11-

C. Assignments and Grades

Course grade

Class participation including group projects or cases	20%
Term paper	40%
Final exam	40%

Term Paper

This should be 10-15 pages in length and relate directly to international banking. Subjects on or off the course outline may be acceptable, but all subjects must be approved in advance. For this purpose, a one page outline is due on Monday, June 9. A list of suggested topics will be distributed.

D. Books

Required

1. D. Gunter Dufey and Ian H. Giddy, The International Money Market (Englewood Cliffs, N.J.:Prentice-Hall, 1978).

2. F. John Mathis, ed., Offshore Lending by U.S. Commercial Banks (Philadelphia: Bankers' Association for Foreign Trade and Robert Morris Associates, 1975)

3. Angelini, Anthony, Maximo Eng and Francis A. Lees, International Lending, Risk and Euromarkets, London, MacMillan, 1979.

4. Columbia Journal of World Business, Fall 1979. Available for $4 from the Case Room.

Recommended

1. Francis Lees, International Banking and Finance (N.Y.: John Wiley and Sons, 1974).(Not bedtime reading, but a standard reference work.)

2. Jane W. Little, Eurodollars: The Money-Market Gypsies (New York: Harper and Row, 1975). (Excellent bedtime reading; stimulating and informative to boot.)

Other Reference Books

1. American Bankers Association, International Banking (Washington, D.C.,1970).

2. James C. Baker and M. Gerald Bradford, American Banks Abroad: Edge Act Companies and Multinational Banking (New York:Praeger,19-)

3. Geoffrey Bell, The Eurodollar Market and the International Financia System (London: MacMillan and Co., 1973).

4. Paul Einzig, Roll-Over Credits (New York: St.Martin's Press, 1973).

5. Paul Einzig and Brian Scott Quinn, <u>The Euro-dollar System</u>, 6th Edition (New York: St.Martin's Press, 1977).

6. Maximo Eng, U.S. <u>Overseas Banking - Its Past, Present and Future</u> (Business Research Institute, St. John's University, 1970).

7. Douglas A. Hayes, <u>Bank Lending Policies: Domestic and International</u> (GSBA, University of Michigan, 1971).

8. Francis A. Lees and Maximo Eng, <u>International Financial Markets</u> (New York: Praeger, 1975).

9. Peter K. Oppenheim, <u>International Banking</u> (2nd ed., New York: American Institute of Banking, 1969).

10. Stuart W. Robinson, Jr., <u>Multinational Banking</u> (Leiden: A.S. Sijthoff, 1972).

11. McKenzie, George W., <u>The Economics of the Euro-Currency System</u>, New York: Wiley & Sons, 1976. (Uses more economic theory than most books on the subject.)

12. Mayer, Martin, <u>The Bankers</u>. A semipopular book available in paperback that has some lively chapters on international banking.

13. Frowen Stephen F., ed., <u>A Framework of International Banking</u>, Guildford, Surrey, U.K., Guildford Educational Press, 1979.

14. Steven Davis, <u>The Management Function in International Banking</u>, Halsted, 1980.

15. Nigel Hudson, <u>Money and Exchange Dealing in International Banking</u>, Halsted, 1980.

16. T.H. Donaldson, <u>Lending in International Commercial Banking</u>, Halsted, 1980.

17. Morris Mendelsohn, <u>Money on the Move</u>, 1980.

The library is just in the process of acquiring these last five books.

E. <u>Periodicals and Sources</u>

Each participant in the course should get on the following free mailing lists.

1. <u>International Letter</u>, Federal Reserve Bank of Chicago, Chicago, Ill., 60690.

2. <u>The Morgan Guaranty Survey</u>, Morgan Guaranty Trust Company, 23 Wall Street, New York, N.Y., 10015

3. <u>Monthly Economic Letter</u>, First National City Bank, 399 Park Avenue, New York, N.Y., 10022.

4. <u>New England Economic Review</u>, Research Department, Federal Reserve Bank of Boston, Boston, Mass., 02106.

The following periodicals contain articles of current interest to international bankers. Probably the single most useful is Euromoney. Students are advised to look through recent issues before the course begins.

1. The American Banker (Daily)
2. The Banker (British)
3. The Bankers' Magazine (British) (Monthly)
4. The Bankers Magazine (American) (Quarterly)
5. The Journal of Commercial Bank Lending
6. Journal of Bank Research
7. Banking
8. The Money Manager
9. The Bankers Monthly
10. The Economist
11. Euromoney
12. World Financial Markets (Morgan Guaranty Trust)
13. Federal Reserve Bank of Chicago Business Conditions
14. Federal Reserve Bank of New York Monthly Review
15. Financing Foreign Operations (Business International Corp.)
16. International Finance (Chase Manhattan Bank)
17. The Financial Times (London)
18. The Wall Street Journal
19. The Financial Post (Toronto)
20. Japan Economic Journal (Weekly in English)
21. Handelsblatt (in German)
22. Banque (in French)
23. Columbia Journal of World Business
24. First Chicago World Report (First National Bank of Chicago)
25. Federal reserve Bulletin

When you are seeking articles or information about a particular topic, company or country, the following indexes and abstracts might prove useful:

1. Business Periodicals Index
2. F & S International
3. Journal of Economic Literature
4. Public Affairs Information Service
5. The Wall Street Journal Index
6. The New York Times Index

The following are useful statistical sources on international finance and banking:

General

1. OECD Financial Statistics (Organization for Economic Cooperation and Development)
2. OECD Industrial Production
3. OECD Main Economic Indicators
4. General Statistics (European Community)
5. Social Statistics (EEC)
6. Agricultural Statistics (EEC)
7. Monthly Bulletin of Statistics (U.N.)
8. International Financial Statistics (International Monetary Fund)
9. Key Figures of European Securities
10. Survey of Current Business (U.S. Department of Commerce)
11. Rates of Change in Economic Data for Ten Industrial Countries (St. Louis Fed.)
12. Central Bank bulletins for most countries
13. Balance of Payments Yearbook (IMF)
14. International Economic Indicators and Competitive Trends (U.S. Dept. of Commerce)

Eurodollars and Eurobonds

1. Euromoney
2. International Bond Guide (White Weld)
3. World Financial Markets
4. Bank for International Settlements Annual Report
5. Borrowing in International Capital Markets (World Bank)
6. Bank of England Quarterly Bulletin
7. The Week in Eurobonds (Kidder, Peabody)
8. Financial Times (London)
9. The Money Manager

Foreign Exchange Rates

1. Bank and Quotation Record (back page)
2. Wall Street Journal
3. Selected Interest and Exchange Rates (Federal Reserve System)
4. Pick's Currency Yearbook
5. Euromoney
6. International Financial Statistics (IMF)

Term Paper

The term paper will comprise 40% of your grade for the course. A
one page outline is due Monday, June 9. Topics may suggest them-
selves from the course outline, or from the lists below. I will
reserve the right to veto topics, but I am open to any idea related
to international banking.

Titles of term papers from Spring 1980

Commercial Bank Lending to LDCs: Effects in pricing

The Reluctant Evolution: The growing role of the Deutsche mark as
    an international reserve asset.

The Political Risk Factor in Commercial Bank Lending to Developing
    Countries

Yen-Denominated Securities Investment for International Banking
    Management

A Case for Foreign Banking in the U.S.

Eurodollars and the Federal Reserve: Monetary Policy and Regulatory
    Response

East Europe's Debt to the West

Debt Renegotiation: Process Mechanisms in the 1978 Peruvian Case

Turkey's Foreign Debts

An Analysis of U.S. Offices of Foreign Banks

The Invasion of the Japanese City Banks into the Syndicated Loan
    Market

LDC Lending

The Establishment, Development and Operation of the Offshore Banking
    Unit in Bahrain

The Edge Act: Its history in U.S. Banking

The International Banking Act of 1978 and the Opportunities for Edge
    Branching

Country Risk Analysis: The Latin American experience

The Asian Dollar Market

Legal Aspects of the Iranian Asset Freeze

The Proposed Bank Act and Its Effects on the Canadian Banking Structure

The Next International Banking Crisis

Recycling Petrodollars

Commercial Banks and the IMF in LDC Lending as Seen Through the
    Peruvian Experience: Their past and present role in LDC Financing

Examination of Certain Consequences of Barriers to Entry and Regulatory Policies Affecting Operations of U.S. Banks in Great Britain, Switzerland, France and West Germany

The Republic of Zaire: A study of indebtedness among less-developed countries

LDC Debt: Is there a real danger?

The Scottish Banking System: A Phoenix in the International Community?

The Operations of the International Monetary Fund and Changing Conditionality Terms

The Eurodollar Markets: Forces which impact on Eurodollar interest rates

Financing China's Future Development

Banking in and with China

Elements of Co-Financing

Developments in Consortium Bank Lending

A Study of Italian Banks in the United States

Additional Suggestions for term papers

Ventures into consumer banking abroad

Regulatory treatment of U.S. Banks abroad

Deposit freezing

Asian dollar market

Determinants of the location of overseas banking

Determinants of the composition of international banking by nationality

International comparison of solvency or other banking regulation

International comparison of banking organizational and industry structure, and/or asset and liability structure

Effects of foreign bank entry (into U.S. or elsewhere) on bank industry structure, and/or organizational structure, balance sheet composition, and regulatory practice.

Eurodollar markets: determinants of interest rates (e.g., premium on Eurodollar deposit rates)

I. Larger Contexts

Weeks 1 and 2

Introduction:

* "Overseas Banking," Chapter 8 in Henning, C.N., Pigott, W. and Scott R.H., _International Financial Management_, New York, McGraw-Hill, 1978.

Lees (1974), Chapters 1-7.

Some banking theory

a. Domestic banking

   Carson, Deane, "Commercial Banks as Financial Intermediaries" and "Government Regulation of Commercial Banks," Chapter 26 and 27 of _Economics_ (manuscript)

b. International banking

   *Aliber, R., "Towards a Theory of International Banking," Federal Reserve Bank of San Francisco, _Review_ Spring 1976

   Dean, James W. and Herbert G. Grubel, "Regulatory Issues and the Theory of Multinational Banking," in Frank R. Edwards, ed., _Issues in Financial Regulation_, N.Y. McGraw-Hill, 1978.

   Ganoe, G., "Internationalization of Commercial Bank Lending," Journal of _Commercial Banking Lending_, May 1974.

   Grubel, Herbert G., "A Theory of Multinational Banking," _Banca Nazionale del Lavoro Quarterly Review_, December 1977.

Some postwar history

a. U.S. banks move abroad

   *Fieleke, Norman S., "The Growth of U.S. Banking Abroad: An Analytical Survey," and comments following by Phalem and Aliber, and reply by Fieleke. In Federal Reserve Bank of Boston, _Key Issues in International Banking_. Proceedings of a conference held in October, 1977, pp. 9-53.

b. Non U.S. banks internationalize

   *Jacobs, K.P., "The Development of International and Multi-national Banking in Europe," _Columbia Journal of World Busine_ Winter, 1975, pp. 33-39.

   *"City of London Survey," _Euromoney_, January 1978, pp. 69, 71, 73, 76, 79, 81, 83-84, 86-87.

   Fallen, P., "Hong Kong Forges Ahead," _Euromoney_, July 1977, pp. 88-92.

c. Foreign banks enter the U.S.

*"Foreign Banks in New York" Euromoney, June 1978, pp. 58-9, 61, 63, 66, 69-70, 72-74, 76-77, 79, 81, 83, 85, 87-88.

"Recent Growth of U.S. Offices of Foreign Banks," Féderal Reserve Bulletin, October 1976

"Foreign Banking in the U.S.: Special Report," Institutional Investor, September 1977.

*Terrell, H.S. and Key, S.J., "The Growth of Foreign Banking in the United States: An Analytical Survey," and comments following by Richard Caves. In Fed. of Boston, op.cit under a. above.

Terrell, H.S. and Key, S.J., "The U.S. Activities of Foreign-Owned Banking Organizations," Columbia Journal of World Business, Winter 1975, pp. 87-97.

Dean, James W. and Ian H.Giddy, "Strangers and Neighbours: Cross-Border Banking in North America," Banca del Lavoro Nazionale Quarterly Review, June or September, 1981.

d. Major International banks today

*"The Winners in 1977," Euromoney, July 1977, pp. 88-92.

"The Top 300," The Banker (London), June 1975, pp. 676-683, 725-733.

Week 3

The Eurocurrency market: first principles

Carson, Dean, "Government Policies and the Eurodollar Market," Columbia Journal of World Business, Winter 1975, pp. 58-64.

*Dufey and Giddy, Chapter 1

*Friedman, Milton, "The Eurodollar Market: Some First Principles," Federal Reserve Bank of St. Louis Review, July 1971. Reprinted in R.E. Baldwin and J.D. Richardson, eds., International Trade and Finance, Boston: Little, Brown, 1974, Chapter 28.

*H. Robert Heller, "Assessing Euromarket Growth: Why the Market is Demand-Determined," Euromoney, February 1979, pp. 41-47.

Klopstock, Fred H., "Money Creation in the Eurodollar Market - A Note on Professor Friedman's Views," in Baldwin and Richardson, ibid.

Klopstock, Fred H., "The Eurodollar Market: Some Unresolved Issues," Princeton Essays in International Finance, No. 65.

Lees (1974), Chapter 11.

*Little, Chapters 2-3

*Giddy, Ian H., "Why Eurodollars Grow," Columbia Journal of World Business, Fall 1979.

Week 4

Credit and liquidity creation by international banks

*Mayer, Helmut, "Credit and liquidity creation in the international banking sector," BIS, Basle, November 1979.

Mayer, Helmut W., "Multiplier Effects and Credit Creation in the Eurodollar Market," Banca Nazionale del Lavoro Quarterly Review, Sept. 1971, pp. 233-62.

Swoboda, Alexander, "The Eurodollar Market: An Interpretation," Princeton Essays in International Finance, No. 64.

*Dufey and Giddy, Chapter 3, Including Appendices.

*Little, Jane S., "Liquidity creation by Eurobanks, a range of possibilities," CJWB, Fall, 1979.

*McClam, Warren D., "US Monetary Aggregates, Income Velocity and the Euro-Dollar Market," BIS, Basle, April 1980.

II. Regulatory Issues

Week 5

Eurodollars and national monetary policy

   *Dufey and Giddy, Chapters 4 & 6.

   *Angelini, Eng and Lees, Chapter 7.

   McKenzie, Chapters,5,6 and 9.

   *Little (1975), Chapters 6,7 and 8.

   *Mayer, Helmut, "The Eurocurrency Market and the Autonomy of U.S. Monetary Policy," CJWB, Fall, 1979.

   *Davis, Robert R., "Effects of the Eurodollar Market on National Monetary Policies," CJWB, Fall 1979.

International banking and international financial intermediation.

   *Llewellyn, David T., "International financial intermediation," Chapter 1 in Frowen, op.cit.

   *Llewellyn, David T., "International banking in the 1970's: an overview," Chapter 2 in Frowen, op.cit.

   *Llewellyn, David T., "A fragile international monetary system," Chapter 3 in Frowen, op.cit.

Hauge, Gabriel and Erik Hoffmeyer, The International Capital Market and the International Monetary System, 1978 Per Jacobsson Lecture, International Monetary Fund, 1978. Monograph included commentary by Lord Roll of Ipsden. On library reserve.

Debs, Richard A., "Petro-Dollars, LDCs, and International Banks," Public address, January 9, 1976. On library reserve.

Weeks 6 & 7

Current regulatory issues

*Giddy, Ian H., "The Public Policy Implications of the Eurocurrency Market," CJWB, Fall, 1979.

*Dean, James W. and Herbert G. Grubel, "Regulatory Issues and the Theory of Multinational Banking," in Frank R. Edwards, ed., Issues in Financial Regulation, N.Y. McGraw-Hill, 1978.

*Aliber, Robert Z., "Monetary Aspects of Offshore Markets, " CJWB, Fall 1979.

*Lees, Chapter 13.

*Frydl, Edward J., "The Debate Over Regulating the Eurocurrency Markets," FRB of NY, Quarterly Review, Winter, 1979-80. (Listed on reserve under "FRB of NY")

*"Why the Fed Fears to Relax its Grip on International Transactions," Euromoney, April 1979, pp. 175, 177, 179.

*Wallich, Henry C., "Central Banks as Regulators and Lenders of Last Resort in an International Context: A View from the United States," in FRB of Boston, op.cit. (Weeks 1 and 2)

McMahon, Christopher W., "Central Banks as Regulators and Lenders of Last Resort in an International Context: A View from the United Kingdom," and comments by Kindleberger. In FRB of Boston, op.cit. (weeks 1 & 2).

Johnson, Robert, "International Banking, Risk, and U.S. Regulatory Policies," FRB of San Francisco Economic Review, Fall 1977.

"Why the Fed. Fears to Relax its Grip on International Transactions," Euromoney April 1979, p. 175. A free trade zone in N.Y. International banking?

Allen B. Frankel, "The Lender of Last Resort Facility in an International Context," Columbia Journal of World Business, Winter 1976.

H.R. Hutton, "The Regulation of Foreign Banks-A European Viewpoint," Columbia Journal of World Business, 1976.

*Wallich, Henry C., "Why the Euromarket Needs Restraint," CJWB, Fall 1979.

*Putnam, Bluford, "Controlling the Euromarkets: A Policy Perspective," CJWB, Fall 1979.

Robert Z. Aliber, "International Banking: Growth and Regulation," Columbia Journal of World Business, Winter 1976.

Andrew F. Brimmer and Frederic B. Dahl, "Growth of American International Banking: Implications for Public Policy," Journal of Finance, Vol. 30, No. 2 (May, 1975), pp. 341-363.

Allen Frankel, "International Banking: Structural Aspects of Regulation," Federal Reserve Bank of Chicago Business Conditions, October 1974, pp. 3-11.

Fred H. Klopstock, "Bye-Bye 'Go-Go' Banking," Banking, June 1975.

Prudential Issues

*Grubel, Herbert G., "A Proposal for the Establishment of an International Deposit Insurance Corporation," _Princeton Essays in International Finance_ No. 133, July 1979.

*Dean, James W. and Ian H. Giddy, "Averting International Banking Crises," _Monograph Series in Finance and Economics_, New York University, 1981, forthcoming.

Dean, James W. and Ian H. Giddy, "Six Ways to World Banking Safety", _Euromoney_, May 1981.

Spero, Joan E., _The Failure of the Franklin National Bank_, Columbia University Press, 1979.

Week 8

Foreign banks in the U.S. and the International Banking Act of 1978

   See also week 2, section c.

*Gulkowitz, Abraham, "Foreign banking in the U.S.- end of the honeymoon," _The Banker_, June 1979. To be distributed.

*Federal Reserve Bulletin, "Implementation of the International Banking Act," October 1979.

*Segala, John P., "A Summary of the International Banking Act of 1978," FRB of Richmond, _Economic Review_, Jan/Feb 1979.

*FRB of Dallas, "Expanded Powers for Edge Act Corporations Proposed by the Fed," _Voice_, April 1979. To be distributed.

*Volcker, Paul A., "Treatment of Foreign Banks in the U.S.: Dilemmas and Opportunities," Remarks before the International Monetary Conference, London, June 12, 1979. To be distributed.

*Statement by Henry C. Wallich before the U.S. Senate Committee on Banking, Housing, and Urban Affairs, July 16, 1979. To be distributed.

Edwards, Franklin R. and Jack Zwick, "Foreign Banks in the United States - Activities and Regulatory Issues," _CJWB_, Spring 1975.

*Dean and Giddy, op.cit., week 2, section c.

III. The International Bank as a Financial Intermediary

Week 9

Sources of funds

   a.   Eurocurrency deposits
        *Potter, "Short-term London Dollar Market Survey," _Euromoney_, August 1977, pp. 66-67, 69-70, 72.

        *Stigum, Marcia, _The Money Market: Myth,Reality and Practice_ New York, Dow Jones-Irwin, 1978, Chapters 15 & 16.

Dufey and Giddy, Chapter 2.

"London Dollar Certificates of Deposit," Appendix 1 in Einzig and Quinn.

Shaw, Ray, "The U.K. money market," in Frowen, Stephen F., A Framework of International Banking, Guildford,Surrey,U.K., Guildford Educational Press, 1979.

Shaw, Ray, "London as a financial centre," in Frowen, ibid.

   b. Liability management

*Dufey and Giddy, Chapter 5, Sections 1 & II.

Mathis, Chapter 12.

Uses of Funds: Overview

"International Bank Lending: A Guided Tour Through the Data," FRB of New York Quarterly Review, Autumn, 1978.

*Angelini, Eng and Lees, Chapter 1.

*Dufey and Giddy, Chapter 5, Section III.

Lees (1974), Chapter 8.

Mathis, Chapter 1.

Dennis, G.E.J., "Statistical analysis of international banking: external bank positions," Chapter 4 in Frowen, ed., op.cit.

Dennis, G.E.J., "Stastical analysis of international banking: external bonds and eurocurrency credits," Chapter 5 in Frowen, ed., op.cit.

Weeks 10,11

Loan practices in international banking

"Lees, Francis A., "International lending strategies of commercial banks," CJWB, Winter, 1976.

   a. Loans to corporations and banks

*Angelini, Eng and Lees, Chapter 2

*Mathis, Chapter 8.

*Mathis, Chapter 10.

Mathis, Chapters 3-5.

Einzig (1973)

   b. Loans to governments

*Angelini, Eng and Lees, Chapter 3.

*Mathis, Chapter 11.

Cheng, Han-Son, "Commercial Bank Financing of World Payments Imbalances," Fed. Res. Bank of San Francisco Economic Review, Fall, 1977.

Lees, (1974), Chapters 10 and 12.

Cleveland, H. and Brittain, W., "Are LDC's in Over Their Heads?" Foreign Affairs, July 1977, pp. 732-50.

Feder, C. and Just, R., "An Analysis of Credit Terms in the Eurodollar Market," European Economic Review, May 1977, pp. 221-43.

Q.P. Lin, "Comecon Debt: A Hectic Year of Borrowing," Euromoney Jan. 1978, pp. 13-15, 17.

Forrest, George and Noel Mills, "Debt analysis and financing problems of developing countries," Chapter 7, Part 1, in Frowen, ed., op.cit., pp. 152-74.

c. Evaluation of risk by country, firm and currency

*Mathis, Chapters 2-4.

Frank, C. and W. Cline, "Measurement of Servicing Capacity," Journal of International Economics, Vol. 1, pp. 327-44.

von Agtmael, A., "Evaluating the Risks of Lending to Developing Countries," Euromoney, April 1976, pp. 16-30.

*Friedman, Irving S., "Evaluation of Risk in International Lending: A Lender's Perspective," and comments by Dornbusch. In Fed of Boston, op.cit. (Weeks 1 and 2).

*Schuler, Harold D., "Evaluation of Risk in International Lending: A Bank Examiner's Perspective," and comments by Grubel and reply by Schuler.

Brittain, W.H. Bruce, "Developing Countries' External Debt and the Private Banks," Banca Nazionale del Lavoro Quarterly Review, Dec. 1977, pp. 385-390.

*Donald R. Mandich, "Pricing International Loans, The Bankers Magazine, Spring, 1971.

John D. Wilson, "Latest Developments in U.S. Bank Loan Pricing," Euromoney, May 1974.

Douglas A. Hayes, Bank Lending Policies: Domestic and International (GSBA, University of Michigan, 1971), last 3 chapters.

P. Henry Mueller, "Sighting in On International Lending," Journal of Commercial Bank Lending, September 1972, pp. 2-19.

Alberto A. Weissmuller, "Assessing the Country Credit Risk," Euromoney, October 1972, pp. 57-59.

J.R. Cummings, "Beware of the Pitfalls of Foreign Financial Lending," Journal of Commercial Bank Lending, July 1972.

C.S. Ganoe, "Internationalization of Commercial Lending," Journal of Commercial Bank Lending, May 1974

*Forrest and Mills, op.cit., Chapter 7, Part 2, pp. 174-85.

In addition, <u>Euromoney</u> carries something on risk evaluation in almost every issue. In 1979, aspects of currency risk were treated in the Jan., May, June, July and Oct. issues. Country risk was treated in the Oct. and Nov. issues, and the Dec. issue carried a good article by a lawyer on "pruning" (i.e. simplifying) loan agreements.

Week 12

Some specialized activities

>Davis, Steven I., "Techniques in international banking," Chapter 6 in Frowen, ed., <u>op</u>.<u>cit</u>.

Syndicated Loans

>*Angelini, Eng and Lees, Chapter 5.

>*Mathis, Chapter 9.

>Einzig, (1973).

>Park, Yoon S., <u>The Eurobond Market: Function and Structure</u>, New York: Praeger, 1974, Chapter 7.

Investment banking and the international bond market

>*Lees (1974), Chapter 9.

>*Yassukovich, Stanislas, "The Development of the International Capital Market," <u>Euromoney</u>, Jan. 1971. pp. 16-20.

>Park, <u>op</u>.<u>cit</u>. (week 7), Chapters 1-6.

Legal aspects of international lending

>*Mathis, Chapter 5.

>*Angelini, Eng and Lees, Chapter 6.

The University of Michigan
Graduate School of Business Administration

International Business/Finance 613

INTERNATIONAL FINANCE -- INTERNATIONAL FINANCIAL MARKETS

Instructor: Professor Gunter Dufey

Fall 1980

The focus of this course is on the international financial environment in which business firms operate. Essentially, it is a "macro"
course; managerial problems are addressed only indirectly. It is
tailored to students looking for careers in international banking,
international institutions, or with the finance departments of corporations operating in world markets.

COURSE OUTLINE AND READING LIST

Text: Wilson E. Schmidt, <u>The U.S. Balance of Payments and the Sinking Dollar</u>,
New York University Press, 1979.

General Reference Books:

1. Robert Z. Aliber (ed.), <u>National Monetary Policies and the International
Financial System</u>, (University of Chicago Press, 1974)

2. Charles A. Coombs, <u>The Arena of International Finance</u> (John Wiley, 1976)

3. Gottfried Haberler, <u>A Survey of International Trade Theory</u> (IFSP, 1961)

4. Ronald I. McKinnon, <u>Money in International Exchange: The Convertible
Currency System</u> (1979).

5. Charles P. Kindleberger, <u>Power and Money</u>, (1970)

6. Charles P. Kindleberger and Peter H. Lindert, <u>Intl. Economics</u>, 6th
edition

7. Mordechai E. Kreinin, <u>International Economics</u>, 3nd Ed. (H.B.J., Inc.,
1975)

8. F.A. Lees and M. Eng, <u>International Financial Markets</u> (Praeger, 1975)

9. Machlup, Salant, Tarshis, <u>International Mobility and Movement of Capital</u>
(NBER, 1972)

10. Gerald M. Meier, <u>Problems of a World Monetary Order</u>, (Oxford U. Press,
1974)

11. Robert A. Mundell, <u>International Economics</u>, (MacMillan, 1968)

12. Robert Solomon, <u>The International Monetary System</u>, (1945-1975)

13. Robert Stern, <u>The Balance of Payments</u>, (Aldine, 1973)

14. Leland B. Yeager, <u>International Monetary Relations</u>, (2nd Edition) (Harper
and Row, 1976)

15. Benjamin J. Cohen, <u>Organizing the World's Money</u>, (Basic Books, 1977)

16. Fred C. Bergsten, <u>Dilemmas of the Dollar: Economics and Politics of the
U.S. International Monetary Policy</u>, (N.Y.U. 1975)

17. Richard M. Levich, <u>The International Money Market</u> (JAI Press, 1979).

18. Brendan Brown, <u>Money Hard and Soft</u> (John Wiley Halsted, 1978).

I. INTERNATIONAL FINANCIAL MARKETS & THE FINANCIAL SYSTEM

    Overview, Concepts

    * Lees and Eng, pp. 3-45

A. THE BASICS

II. THE "REAL" SIDE OF INTERNATIONAL FINANCE - A REVIEW

    * Heller, International Monetary Economics, Chapter 1

    If confused, work also through one or more of the following sources:

      Kindleberger, Chapters 2, 3, 4
      Root, Chapters 2, 3 (IB 510 Textbook)
      Kreinin, Chapter 11

III. BALANCE OF PAYMENTS ANALYSIS

    **Dufey/Mirus, International Transactions Summarized: The B/P
    (Teaching Note #2)

    *Schmidt, Chapters I and II

    Schmidt, Appendix A and B to Chapter II.

IV. THE BASIC ADJUSTMENT PROCESS

    **Dufey/Mirus, The Adjustment Process (Teaching Note #3) including
    Appendix A

    * Schmidt, Chapter III

    In addition, read one of the following:

      Kindleberger, Chapters 19, 20, 21, 22
      Kreinin, Chapters 4, 5, 6
      Root, Chapters 9, 10

    Marina v. N. Whitman, "Global Monetarism: Theory, Policy, and
    Critique," Journal of Portfolio Management, Spring 1977.

Note: Readings marked with an * are considered essential.

**Items are in Readings package.

V. ECONOMIC GROWTH & THE BALANCE OF TRADE

   **Dufey/Mirus, "Economic Growth & the Balance of Trade," Appendix B to
   Teaching Note #3.

   W.M. Corden, Recent Developments in the Theory of International Trade
   IFSP, 1965
   Kindleberger and Lindert, Chapters 4,5
   Stern, Chapter 11

B.   INTL. FINANCIAL MARKETS

VI. SHORTTERM INTERNATIONAL FINANCIAL MARKETS: INSTITUTIONS & THEORY

   A. The Foreign Exchange Market

      **Dufey/Mirus, "The Market for Foreign Exchange" (Teaching Note #5)
      * Dealing with $150 Million a Day, International Management, January
      1975, pp. 30-34
      Roger M. Kubarych, Foreign Exchange Markets in the United States,
      Fed. Res. Bank of New York 1978
      H. Riehl and R.M. Rodriquez, Foreign Exchange Markets, New York 1977
      D.R. Mandich (ed.), Foreign Exchange Trading Techniques and Controls,
      ABA 1976

   B. National and External Money Markets

      * Dufey/Giddy, The International Money Market (PH, 1978) Chapters 1,
      2, 3, 4, skip Appendices.
      Jane Sneddon Little, "The Impact of the Eurodollar Market..." The New
      England Economic Review (Fed. Res. Bank of Boston), March-April
      1975, pp. 3-19
      Helmut W. Mayer, Credit and Liquidity Creation in the International
      Banking Sector, BIS Economic Paper No. 8, Nov. 1979.
      Jane S. Little, Eurodollars--The Money Market Gypsies, New York 1975
      E.J. Frydl, "The Debate over Regulating the Eurocurrency Market,
      FRBNY Quarterly Review, Winter 79-80.

   C. Theory and Applicatons

      * Dufey/Mirus The Theory of Intl. Interest and Exchange Rates
         (Teaching Note #7)

VII. LONGTERM CAPITAL MARKETS

      * Dufey/Mirus, "Internatonal Diversification of Investment
      Portfolios" (Teaching Note #8)
      M.E. Polakoff et. al., Financial Institutions and Markets, 1970
      (Chapter 18)
      G. Dufey, The Eurobond Market: Functon and Future, University of
      Washington, 1969
      Y.S. Park, The Eurobond Market: Function and Structure, Praeger,
      1975

* OECD, The Market for International Issues, Paris, OECD 1972
  Susan B. Foster, "Impact of Direct Investment Abroad by United
  States Multinational Companies on the Balance of Payments,"
  Federal
  Reserve Bank of New York, Monthly Review, July 1972, pp. 166-0177
* Giorgio Ragazzi, "Theories and Determinants of Direct Foreign
  Investment" IMF STaff Papers, 1973, pp. 471-498
** G. Dufey, A Study of International Capital Markets, unpublished
  April, 1980.

   C.   THE POLITICAL ECONOMY OF INTERNATIONAL FINANCE

VIII.   CAPITAL CONTROLS AND MARKET INTEGRATION

                    NOTE ON CONTROLS
* Case Study: The U. S. Capital Control Program 1965-74 (handout)
  J.M. Hessels, "Prospects and Problems of an Integrated European
    Securities Market," Euromoney, March 1973, pp. 4-8.

"The Year of the Barriers," The Economist, Jan. 27, 1973, pp. 9-26 of
    survey

John Mellors, "Multinational Corporations and Capital Market
    Integration," Proceedings, Fourth Colliquium of Societe
    Universitaire Europeenne de Recherches Financieres (SUERF)
    Nottingham University, April 1973

Peter B. Kenen, Capital Mobility and Financial Integration: A Survey
    Princeton Studies in International Finance #39, 1976, pp. 1-34
    only

IX.   THE EVOLUTION OF THE INTERNATIONAL MONETARY SYSTEM

* Dufey/Mirus, "The Organization and Working of the International
    Financial System" (Teaching Note #4)

W.M. Scammell, International Monetary Policy - Bretton Woods & After,
    Macmillan, 1975

Gerald M. Meier (see general reference books)

Charles A. Coombs (see general reference books)

* Harry Johnson, "Toward a World Central Bank," The Banker, Feb.
    1976, p. 137-139

  Samuel I. Katz, "'Managed Floating' As an Interim International Ex-
    change Rate Regime, 1973-1975," The Bulletin, New York
    University-GSBA, 1975/3.

* R. Dornbush, "What Have We Learned from the Float," unpublished,
    Feb. 24, 1977

W. M. Corden, Monetary Integration, Essays in International Finance,
    Princeton, No. 93, April 1972

* "The Commercial Use of SDR's", World Financial Markets, Morgan
    Guaranty Trust Co., August 4, 1975, pp. 4-11.

**Peter M. Oppenheimer, Origins and Prospects, unpublished, Oxford,
    May, 1979.

X.   LDCs AND INTERNATIONAL FINANCE

R.I. McKinnon, Money and Capital in Economic Development, Brookings,
    1973, pp. 5-19, 170-177

* Ismail S. Abdalla, "Bringing Democracy Into the World Monetary
    System" Euromoney, April 1977

* A.G. Chandavarkar, "How Relevant is Finance for Development,"
    Finance and Development, Sept. 1973, Vol. 10, No. 3, pp. 14-16.

**Kredietbank, "A country's Credit Status," Weekly Bulletin, No. 21,
    1980.

William R. Cline, International Monetary Reform and the Developing
    Countries, Brookings, 1976, esp. pp. 108-112

*G. Dufey, and S. Min, The Access of Developing Countries to
    International Credit, The University of Michigan, GSBA Working
    Paper 148, July 1977, esp. pp. 18-31.

*John Dizard, "The Revolution in Assessing Country Risk,"
    Institutional Investor (International Edition), Oct. 1978, pp. 65

XI.   OPEC AND THE INTERNATIONAL FINANCIAL SYSTEM

Thomas D. Willett, The Oil Transfer Problem and International
    Economic Stability, Essays in International Finance, Princeton,
    Dec. 1975, No. 113

S.J. Kobrin and D.R. Lessard, "Large Scale OPEC Investment in
    Industrialized Countries and the Theory of Foreign Direct
    Investment - A Contradiction?" M.I.T. Working Paper 786-75 (XBA
    3195 No. 786-1975)

Gottfried Haberler, "Oil, Inflation, Recession and the International
    Monetary System," AEI Reprint No. 45, June 1976.

XII.   WORLD ECONOMIC ORDER

Marina v. N. Whitman, Sustaining the International Economic System:
    Issues for U.S. Policy, Essays in International Finance,
    Princeton No. 121, June 1977

T. D. Willett, Our Evolving International Economic System, U.S.
    Department of the Treasury, OASIA, Discussion Paper Series, 1977

Gottfried Haberler, "Reflections on the U.S. Trade Deficit and the
    Floating Dollar," in AEI, Contemporary Economic Problems 78, (Wm.
    Fellner, ed.)

The University of Michigan
Graduate School of Business Administration

International Business/Finance 620

FINANCIAL MANAGEMENT IN THE INTERNATIONAL CORPORATION

Instructor: Professor Gunter Dufey

Winter 1981

The focus of this course is on the specific problems encountered
by those concerned with finance in companies with substantial
international involvement. It is the international equivalent
of a corporate finance course (in contrast to a course that
deals with international financial markets).

The course content is especially designed for MBA's aspiring
to careers in financial management of large and small corporations, international trading companies, or banks whose customers
include business firms affected by international markets.

Selected Bibliography

Text   D.K. Eiteman and A.I. Stonehill Multinational Business Finance, 2nd., Ed.
     (Addison-Wesley, 1979)

Recommended Supplementary Text

R.S. Carlson, et. al., International Finance: Cases and Simulation,
(Addison-Wesley, 1980)

Donald R. Lessard, International Financial Management (WGL 1979)

General Reference Books

1.   Peter J. Buckley and Mark Casson, The Future of Multinational Enterprise,
    (Holmes and Meier, New York 1976)

2.   Robert Z. Aliber, Exchange Risk and Corporate International Finance, (Halsted
    1979).

3.   R. M. Rodriguez and E. E. Carter, second ed., International Financial Managem
    Prentice-Hall, 1979 (R & C)

4.   S. M. Robbins and R. B. Stobaugh, Money in the Multinational Enterprise,
    (Basic Books, Inc. 1973)

5.   M. Z. Brooke and H. L. Remmers, The Strategy of Multinational Enterprises, Se
    Edition (Pitman, 1978)

6.   Surendra S. Singhvi, Corporate Financial Management in a Developing
    Economy (University of Washington, Graduate School of Business
    Administration 1972)

7.   Henning, Pigott and Scott, International Financial Management, (McGraw Hill
    1978)

8.   David A. Ricks, International Dimensions of Corporate Finance, (Prentice
    Hall 1978)

9.   Frederick D. S. Choi and Gerhard G. Mueller, An Introduction to
    Multinational Accounting, (Prentice Hall 1978)

10. Laurent L. Jacque, Management of Foreign Exchange Risk, (Lexington Books, 197

11. E. C. Bursk, J. Deardon, D. F. Hawkins and U. M. Longstreet, Financial
    Control of Multi-National Operations (The Research Foundation of
    Financial Executives Institute 1971)

12. Robert Z. Aliber, The International Money Game, third edition, (Basic Books
    1979)

13. Financial Executives Institute, Accounting for the Multinational
    Corporation, (FERF 1978)

14. T.W. McRae and David P. Walker, <u>Foreign Exchange Management</u> (Prentice Hall International, 1980)

15. David B. Zenoff, <u>Management Principles for Finance in the Multinational</u> (Euromoney Publications, 1980)

16. David A. Ricks (ed.), <u>International Financial Management: A Survey of Research Trends and An Annotated Bibliography 1968-76</u> (College of Business Administration, The Ohio State University, Working Paper 77-11, June 1977)

SCHEDULE AND OUTLINE

Date	Topics	Reading List Ref #	Case
	The International Financial Environment - A Comprehensive Review -	1	
	The International Company	2	
	The Finance Function and Int'l Financial Management	3	
	Export Financing; Export Credit Insurance	4	
	Financing East-West Transactions	5	
	Foreign Direct Investment-Strategy & Tactics	6	
	Cash Flow Analysis for Int'l Capital Expenditures	7	
	Taxation of Int'l Operations/General Principles	8	
	Exchange Risk (Operations)	9	
	Risk Analysis Incl. Methods of Project Analysis	10	
	(Exam #1) Capital Structure Decisions in Int'l Companies	11	
	Funding in Int'l Markets, including Exchange Risk and Financing: Strategic Considerations	12	
	Foreign Exchange-Risk & Capital Structure of Financial Institutions	12a	
	Working Capital Management, Transfer Pricing	13	
	Swaps and Interest Arbitrage	14	
	International Cash Management Systems	15	
	Relations with Banks and Other Financial Institutions	16	
	Using Int'l and Foreign Capital Markets	17	
	International Financial Institutions	18	
	Disputes with Host Countries: Financial Aspects	19	
	Financial Reporting and Control (Internal)	20	
	Financial Reporting and Control (External)	21	

Date	Topics	Reading List Ref #	C.
	Organizational Implementation; Review	22	
	Final Examination		

OUTLINE AND READING LIST

Topic #

1   THE INTERNATIONAL FINANCIAL ENVIRONMENT - A COMPREHENSIVE REVIEW

- *E & S, Chapter 2, Foreign Exchange Rate Determination

- R: Z. Aliber, The International Money Game, (2rd edition, 1979) Chapters 1-10

    or

- Leland B. Yeager, The International Monetary Mechanism, esp. Chapters 1, 2, 5, 8

    or

- any other short volume reviewing the international financial system

2   THE INTERNATIONAL COMPANY

- *Sanford, Rose, "The Rewarding Strategies of Multinationalism"   *
Fortune, September 15, 1968

- #5, Chapter 1

3   THE FINANCE FUNCTION AND INTERNATIONAL FINANCIAL MANAGEMENT

- *E & S, Chapter 1, The Scope of Multinational Business Finance

- *S. M. Robbins and R. B. Stobaugh, "Multinational Companies -   *
Growth of the Financial Function," Financial Executive, July 1973,
pp. 24-31

- *G. Dufey, "International Financial Management", Chapter 7 in The *
International Firm, M. Z. Brooke and L. Remmers, Pitman London 1977

- *Lessard, pp. 349-365, The Environment of FMIO - Overview

- E & S, Chapter 5, Financial Goals of MNC

- #4, Chapters 2, 3

Note: A general text on corporate finance might serve as a very useful reference. The following are especially recommended: Van Horne, Financial
Management and Policy. (4th ed.) (Prentice Hall 1977) and/or Weston and
Brigham, Managerial Finance, (6th ed.) (Holt, Rinehart and Winston
(1978).

* required reading - to be done prior to the class meeting
# refers to general reference books

4.   EXPORT FINANCING; EXPORT CREDIT INSURANCE SYSTEMS

- *E&S, Chapter 14, Import and Export Financing

- *Morgan Guaranty, <u>The Financing of Exports and Imports - A Guide to Procedures</u> (or any similar booklet showing export financing procedures)

- *T. Teichman, "Forfaiting," <u>The Banker</u>, March 1977   *

- Credit Suisse, <u>Forfaiting</u>, CS Special Publication, vol. 47II, 1978
- Business International, <u>Financing Foreign Operations</u> (referred to as
- <u>FFO</u>), "Export Financing"

5. FINANCING EAST-WEST TRANSACTIONS

- *Gunter Dufey, "Financing East-West Business" <u>Columbia Journal of</u>   ::
<u>World Business</u>, (Spring 1974)

6. FOREIGN DIRECT INVESTMENT-STRATEGY & TACTICS

- *E&S, Chapter 7, The Foreign Investment Decision

- *Lessard, pp. 19-81, "Direct Investment"

- *R. D. Robinson, "Ownership Strategy," Chapter 5 in <u>International Business Management</u>, (Holt, Rinehart 1978)

- Ian H. Giddy, "The Demise of the Product Cycle Model...." <u>CJWB</u>, (Spring 1978), pp. 90-97

- John M. Stopford and Louis T. Wells, <u>Managing the Multinational Enterprise</u>, (Basic Books 1972), Chapters 7-9

- G.R. Young and S. Bradford, Jr., <u>Joint Ventures: Planning and Action</u>, FEI, 1977.

- #5, Chapter 8, Capital Budgeting

- John Kitching, "Winning and Losing with European Acquisitions" <u>HBR</u>, March-April 1974, pp. 124-36

- Brent D. Wilson, "Foreign Divestment," <u>Multinational Business</u>, No. 2, 1978 pp. 1-11

- "Foreign Investment in the USA," <u>Multinational Business</u>, No. 2, 1978 pp. 12-19

7. CASH FLOW ANALYSIS FOR INTERNATIONAL CAPITAL EXPENDITURES

*#3 Chapter 10   *

*E&S, Chapter 8, "Capital Budgeting"

*Lessard, pp. 565-576, "Evaluating Foreign Cash Flows

Topic #

8. TAXATION OF INTERNATIONAL OPERATIONS – GENERAL PRINCIPLES

   - *Edward P. Parles, "A Guide Through the Tax Maze I & II, Euromoney, Oct. & Nov., 1980.

   - E&S, Chapter 16, Tax Planning

   - Lessard, pp. 517-530, "American Taxation of MNC's"

   - J.D. R. Adams and J. Whalley, The International Taxation of Multinational Enterprises in Developed Countries, Greenwood Press, 1977

9. EXCHANGE RISK (OPERATIONS)

   - *G. Dufey, "Corporate Foreign Exchange Risk: Definitions and Measurements

   - *E&S, Chapter 3, Foreign Exchange Exposure

   - Lessard, pp. 381-407, "Foreign Exchange Risk Exposure"

   - Lessard, pp. 409-442, "Accounting for Exchange Fluctuations"

10. RISK ANALYSIS INCL. METHODS OF PROJECT ANALYSIS

   - *Robert B. Stobaugh, "How to Analyze Foreign Investment Climates" HBR, Sept.-Oct. 1969

   - D.J. Oblak and Roy J. Helm, Jr., "Survey and Analysis of Capital Budgeting Methods Used by Multinationals," Financial Management, Winter 1980, pp. 37-41

   - *Lessard, pp. 577-592, "Evaluating Foreign Projects..."

11. CAPITAL STRUCTURE DECISIONS IN INTERNATIONAL COMPANIES

   - *E&S, Chapter 10, Cost of Capital and Financial Structure

   - *Alan C. Shapiro, "Financial Structure and Cost of Capital in the Multinational Corporation" JFQA, June 1978, pp. 211-226

   - *Lessard, pp. 593-602, "Financing and the Cost of Capital"

   - *FFO, pp. 15-20d, International Guarantees

Topic #

      - *William Hall, " The Fashionable World of Project Finance," The   *
Banker, Jan. '76, pp. 71.

      - Business International, Determining a Worldwide Debt/Equity Policy,
Management Monograph No. 57, 1972.

12. FUNDING IN INTL. MARKETS, INCLUDING EXCHANGE RISK AND FINANCING:
    STRATEGIC CONSIDERATIONS

(12a. FOREIGN EXCHANGE RISK & CAPITAL STRUCTURE IN FINANCIAL INSTITUTIONS)

      - *G. Dufey and I. H. Giddy: "International Financial Planning: The
Use of Market-Based Forecasts", California Management Review, Fall   *
1978

      - *Gail Lieberman, "A Systems Approach to Foreign Exchange   *
Management" Financial Executive, December 1978, pp. 14-19.

      - Ian Giddy, "Exchange Risk - Whose View?" Financial Management,   *
Summer 1977, pp. 33

      - *J.B. Giannotti and D.P. Walker, "How the New FAS 8 Will Change
Exposure Management," Euromoney, Nov. 1980, pp. 111-113.   *

      - *Lessard, pp. 366-330, "The Relevancy of Hedging"

      - Robert C. Bradshaw, "Foreign Exchange Operations of U.S. Banks, "
U.S. Federal Reserve Board of Governors, K.7 Intl. Finance Discussion
Papers, No. 69, Nov. 1975

13. WORKING CAPITAL MANAGEMENT, TRANSFER PRICING,

14. SWAPS & INTEREST ARBITRAGE

      - *E&S, Chapter 4, Reacting to Foreign Exchange Risk

      - *E&S, Chapter 11, Positioning of Funds

      - *#4, Chapter 5,6

      - Lessard, pp. 475-545, "Taxes, Transfer Prices..."

      - V. Victor Suhar and Douglas D. Lyons "Choosing Between a Parallel
Loan and a Swap", Euromoney, March 1979, pp. 114-119

      - J. R. Dempsey, "The Mexican Back-to-Back Loan", Euromoney, May
1978

      - J. R. Dempsey, "Pesos or Dollars in Mexico", Euromoney, June 1978

20. FINANCIAL REPORTING AND CONTROL (INTERNAL)

- *E&S, Chapter 15, Accounting and Evaluation of Performance

- *Lessard, pp. 547-564, "Measuring Performance"

- *Alan C. Shapiro, "Evaluation and Control of Foreign Operations," *
unpublished 1977

- William Person and Van Lessing, <u>Evaluating the Financial
Performance of Overseas Operations</u>, FERF, N.Y., 1979.

- #11, relevant parts only

- #9, Chapter 8

21. FINANCIAL REPORTING AND CONTROL (EXTERNAL)

- #9, Chapters 2, *3, *4, 5, 6

22. ORGANIZATIONAL IMPLEMENTATION AND REVIEW

- *R. G. Bardsley, "The Treasurer's Problems in a Multinational   *
Corporation," <u>Euromoney</u>, May 1975, pp. 76,79

- *Andreas R. Prindl, "Financial Management in the Multinationals," *
<u>Euromoney</u>, April 1975, pp. 70-73

- *A. W. Clements, "The Treasurer's Problems in a Multinational ·   *
Corporation," <u>Euromoney</u>, January 1976, pp. 86-90

(FINAL EXAMINATION)

GEORGETOWN UNIVERSITY

SCHOOL OF BUSINESS ADMINISTRATION

International Finance
Course Number: 1-138-250-01

1981 Spring Semester
Tuesday 6:15-8:45 PM, Walsh 294

Ian H. Giddy
Associate Professor

A. Course Content

This course is designed for those seeking a career in international
finance or banking. Prospective international businessmen or government
officials or pumpkin farmers should also find it interesting. The course
has three segments. First we survey the international financial system,
including the workings of the international credit and foreign exchange
markets and international economic policy and institutions. Next, we move
on to managerial techniques: exchange rate forecasting, exchange risk
management, investment and financing decisions. Finally we look at the
world of international banking. The Eurocurrency market, competitive among
international banks, banking crises and regulatory aspects.

The course will consist of 14 lecture/discussion sessions; we will
also use a few cases and have the occasional guest speaker.

The objective of the course is that you emerge with some analytical
tools to enable you to tackle financial problems in an international context.

B. Assignments and Grades

Distribution of grades

    Class participation. 20%
    Final exam. 80%

Each participant is expected to attend every class session well prepared
for discussion and critique of the readings and cases.

Your performance in class will be judged on (1) the depth of your
preparations of cases, (2) your ability to relate the assigned readings
to management issues found in specific cases, (3) your ability to articulate
your views and analyses, and (4) your ability to listen to fellow students'
viewpoints and build your presentations on them.

The final exam will be a two-hour closed-book, anonymously graded test
of skills and knowledge and your ability to communicate them. Possible
questions will be handed out in advance.

I would like to get to know you. To this end a 3 x 5 index card will
be given out in the first class to each student. All the students must turn
in his/her card on the front side of the card. Any student who fails to
turn in this card by the third class will be deemed to have withdrawn.

1. Name, address, telephone number, student ID number and nationality.

2. Your status in school plus school affiliation.

3. Area of concentration and interest.

4. Educational background (e.g. college attended) and subjects studied.

5. Work experience..

6. Irrelevant information.

C. Background

The course draws heavily on the principles of international economics and of finance. Recommended background preparation is an introductory textbook on financial management and one on international economics or finance. I recommend:

> R.Z. Aliber, <u>The International Money Game</u> (Paperback) 2nd ed.
> or
> Brendan Brown, <u>Money Hard and Soft</u> (Halsted Press, 1978).
> or
> Andrew Crockett, <u>International Money</u> (Academic Press, 1977)

To learn about the foreign exchange markets, I strongly recommend:

> Roger M. Kubarych, <u>Foreign Exchange Markets in the United States</u> (Federal Reserve Bank of New York, 1978)

D. Textbooks

The required textbooks are:

1. David K. Eiteman and Arthur I. Stonehill, <u>Multinational Business Finance</u>: (Addison-Wesley: 2nd ed., 1979).

2. Robert S. Carlson, et al., <u>International Finance: Cases and Simulation</u> (Addison-Wesley, 1980)

Recommended books:

1. Donald Lessard, ed., <u>International Financial Management</u> (Warren, Gorham and Lamont, 1979). A more advanced book of readings.

2. Gunter Dufey and Ian Giddy, <u>The International Money Market</u> (Prentice-Hall, 1978). All about Eurodollars.

3. Rita Rodriguez and Eugene Carter, <u>International Financial Management</u> (Prentice-Hall: 2nd ed., 1979). An alternative to the Eiteman and Stonehill textbook.

E. Other books on international finance, international banking, and international financial management:

1. Ronald McKinnon, Money in International Exchange (Oxford Univ. Press, 1979).

2. Robert Z. Aliber, Exchange Risk and Corporate International Finance, (Halsted Press, 1978).

3. Angelini, Anthony, et. al. International Lending, Risk and the Euromarkets (MacMillan, 1979).

4. F. John Mathis, ed. Offshore Lending by U.S. Commercial Banks , (BAFT and RMA, 1975).

5. Jane S. Little, Eurodollars: The Money-Market Gypsies (Harper and Row, 1975).

6. Stephen F. Frowen, ed., A Framework of International Banking (Guilford Educational Press, 1979).

7. Steven Davis, The Management Function in International Banking (Halsted, 1980)

8. Nigel Hudson, Money and Exchange Dealing in International Banking (Halsted, 1980).

9. T.H. Donaldson, Lending in International Commercial Banking (Halsted, 1980)

10. Morris Mendelsohn, Money on the Move (1980).

11. Herbert G. Grubel, International Economics (Irwin, 1977).

12. Charles Henning, William Pigott and Robert Scott, International Financial Management (New York: McGraw-Hill, 1978).

13. Brendan Brown, Money Hard and Soft, (New York: Wiley, 1978).

14. Laurent Jacque, Management of Foreign Exchange Risk (Lexington Books, 1978).

15. John Heywood, Foreign Exchange and the Corporate Treasurer (Levittown: Transatlantic Arts, 1978).

16. David B. Zenoff and Jack Zwick, International Financial Management (Prentice-Hall, 1969).

17. S.M. Robbins and R.B. Stobaugh, Money in the Multinational Enterprises (Basic Books Inc., 1973).

18. W.A.P. Manser, The Financial Role of Multi-National Enterprises (Associated Business Programmes Ltd., 1973).

19. M.Z. Brooke and H.L. Remmers, The Strategy of Multinational Enterprises (American Elsevier Publishing Company, 1970).

20. Arthur I. Stonehill, Readings in International Financial Management (Goodyear Publishing Company, 1970).

21. E. C. Bursk, J. Deardon, D. F. Hawkins and U.M. Longstreet, Financial Control of Multi-National Operations (The Research Foundation of Financial Executives Institute, 1971).

22. F.A. Lees, International Banking and Finance (New York: Wiley, 1974).

23. Sune Carlson, International Financial Decisions (Amsterdam: North-Holland, 1969).

24. Fred Chol and Gary Meuller, Multinational Accounting and Finance (Prentice-Hall).

25. Rita Rodriguez and Heinz Riehl, Foreign Exchange Markets (New York: McGraw-Hill, 1977).

26. A.R. Prindl, Foreign Exchange Risk, (Wiley, 1976).

27. Richard Ensor and Boris Antl, The Management of Foreign Exchange Risk (London: Euromoney Publications, 1978).

Recent Bibliographies of International Business and Finance:

1. Michael Z. Brooke et al. (eds.), A Bibliography of International Business (London: Macmillan, 1977).

2. Virod B. Bavishi et al. (eds.), International Financial Management- Survey and Bibliography 1973-1976 (Ohio State University College of Administrative Science Working Paper No. 77-22, June 1977).

3. Sanjay Lall, Foreign Private Manuracturing Investment and Multinational Corporations: An Annotated Bibliography (New York: Praeger, 1975).

F. PERIODICALS

The following periodicals contain articles of current interest to international financial managers.

1. Financial Management

2. Financial Analysts Journal

3. Multinational Business

4. The Banker (British)

5. California Management Review

6. Harvard Business Review

7. The Money Manager

8. Business Week

9. Financial Executive

10. The Economist

11. Euromoney

12. World Financial Markets (Morgan Guaranty Trust)
13. Federal Reserve Bank of Chicago Business Conditions
14. Federal Reserve Bank of New York Monthly Review
15. Financing Foreign Operations (Business International Corp.)
16. International Finance (Chase Manhattan Bank)
17. The Financial Times (London)
18. The Wall Street Journal
19. The Financial Post (Toronto)
20. Japan Economic Journal (Weekly in English)
21. Handelsblatt (in German)
22. Banque (in French)
23. Columbia Journal of World Business
24. First Chicago World Report (First National Bank of Chicago).
25. Business International
26. Business Europe (BI)
27. Business Asia (BI)
28. Business Latin America (BI)
29. The Arab Economist
30. Oriental Economist
31. Far Eastern Economic Review
32. Vision (a European Business magazine; in English)
33. Investing, Licensing and Trading (BI)
34. Business International Money Report
35. The Institutional Investor - International Edition
36. International Currency Review

When you are seeking articles or information about a particular topical company or country, the following indexes and abstracts might prove helpful:

1. Business Periodicals Index
2. F. & S. International
3. Journal of Economic Literature
4. Public Affairs Information Service
5. The Wall Street Journal Index
6. The New York Times Index

The following are useful statistical sources on international finance.

General

1. OECD Financial Statistics (Organization for Economic Cooperation and Development)
2. OECD Industrial Production
3. OECD Main Economic Indicators
4. General Statistics (European Economic Community)
5. Social Statistics (EEC)
6. Agricultural Statistics (EEC)
7. Monthly Bulletin of Statistics (U.N.)
8. International Financial Statistics (International Monetary Fund)
9. Key Figures of European Securities
10. Survey of Current Business (U.S. Department of Commerce)
11. Rates of Change in Economic Data for Ten Industrial Countries (St. Louis Fed.)
12. Central Bank bulletins for most countries.
13. Balance of Payments Yearbook (IMF)
14. International Economic Indicators and Competitive Trends (U.S. Dept. of Commerce)
15. U.S. International Transactions and Currency Review (St. Louis Fed.)
16. Government Finance Statistics Yearbook (IMF)

Eurodollars and Eurobonds

1. Euromoney
2. International Bond Guide (White Weld)
3. World Financial Markets
4. Bank for International Settlements Annual Report
5. Borrowing in International Capital Markets (World Bank)
6. Bank of England Quarterly Bulletin
7. The Week in Eurobonds (Kidder, Peabody)
8. Financial Times (London)
9. The Money Manager

Foreign Exchange Rates and Interest Rates

1. Bank and Quotation Record (back page)
2. Wall Street Journal
3. Selected Interest and Exchange Rates (Federal Reserve System)
4. Pick's Currency Yearbook
5. Euromoney
6. International Financial Statistics (IMF)
7. World Currency Charts (American International Investment Corp.)
8. Federal Reserve Bulletin
9. Annual REport on Exchange Restrictions (International Monetary Fund)
10. International Monetary Market Yearbook (Chicago Mercantile Exchange)

U.S. Firms' International Investments

1. Survey of Current Business (U.S. Dept. of Commerce)

Course Outline and Reading List

1. Introduction: International Finance, the Multinational Enterprise, and you

1/20
   Outline of course; tasks of international financial manager and international banker; personal international finance; the international financial
system and the risks and opportunities faced by international firms;
effects of an exchange rate change on prices, income, interest rates, etc.;
avenues to balance of payments adjustment by countries.

   Case: "The Snake" (in-class analysis)

   Readings
* 1. Eiteman and Stonehill, Ch. 5 "The New Hero of American Business,"
      Euromoney, March 1979.

   2. H. R. Heller, International Monetary Economics, Ch. 6-8, 11, 12.

   3. R.Z. Aliber, The International Money Game, 2nd ed., Ch. 1-9.

   4. "Glossary" of international finance terms, in Henning, Pigott
      and Scott, International Financial Management, pp. 553-566.

   5. Dan Throop Smith, "Financial Variables in International Business,"
      Harvard Business Review, Jan. 1966. Also in Stonehill, ed.,
      Readings in International Financial Management.

6. Richard H. Kaufman, "Assessing the International Financial
    Environment," in Sethi and Sheth, eds., <u>Multinational Business
    Operations: Financial Management.</u>

2. International Interest Rates, Exchange Rates and Inflation

1/27

Exchange rate as a price; balance of trade and elasticities; balance
of payments and government intervention; the monetary approach to the
exchange rate.

Money supply and prices; prices and exchange rates (PPP); spot rates,
forward rates and interest rates (IRPT); interest rates and exchange rates
(International Fisher effect); deviations <u>ex ante</u> and <u>ex post</u>.

<u>Case:</u> Eiteman and Stonehill, exs. 2.3, 2.6.

Readings

* 1. Eiteman and Stonehill, Ch. 2

2. Robert Z. Aliber, <u>Exchange Risk and Corporate International Finance</u>
    (Halsted Press, 1978), Ch. 2 "Changes in Exchange Rates as
    Economic Disturbances," and Ch. 3, "Exchange Risk and Yield
    Differentials."

3. Herbert Grubel, <u>International Economics</u> (Irwin, 1977), Ch. 11
    (Ch. 10 optional)

4. Thomas Humphrey and Thomas Lawler, "Factors Determining Exchange
    Rates: A Simple Model and Some Empirical Tests," <u>Federal Reserve
    Bank of Richmond Monthly Review</u> (May/June 1977), 10-15.

5. Gunter Dufey and Ian Giddy, "International Financial Planning;
    The Use of Market-Based Forecasts" <u>California Management Review</u>
    (Fall 1978), 69-81.

6. Roger M. Kubarych, <u>Foreign Exchange Markets in the United States</u>
    (Federal Reserve Bank of New York, 1978), Ch. 3.

3. Foreign Exchange and Eurocurrency Trading

2/3

The nature of a foreign exchange/Euro trading desk; instruments and
contracts traded; spot-forward-euro relationships; arbitrage and speculative profits; links to domestic money markets; actors; brokers and dealers,
banks and corporations, central banks; the international payments clearing
system.

* AN ASTERISK DESIGNATES REQUIRED READING

Readings

*   1.   Roger M. Kubarych, Foreign Exchange Trading in the United States
         (Federal Reserve Bank of New York, 1978) pp. 4-34.

    2.   Nigel Hudson, Money and Exchange Dealing in International Banking
         (Halsted, 1980)

    3.   Marcia Stigum, The Money Market: Myth, Reality and Practice
         (Dow Jones-Irwin, 1978), Ch. 15, 16.

    4.   Paul Erdman, The Billion Dollar Sure Thing (paperback novel).

    5.   Rita Rodriguez and Eugene Carter, International Financial
         Management, Ch. 5 (Try the exercises on pp. 113-114)

4.   Exchange Rate Forecasting

2/10
     What determines exchange rate changes in the short run and in the long
run? Fundamental analysis; forecasting services; the random walk approach;
fixed versus floating rates; the nature of the foreign exchange market
and anticipatory price setting;

Case: "The Mexican Peso, or Wistful Memories of the Good Times." On the
        basis of the data given, try to forecast the direction, amount and
        timing of future changes in the peso's value.

Readings

*1. Robert B. Shulman, "Are Foreign Exchange Risks Measurable?" Columbia
     Journal of World Business, May-June 1970, 55-60.

*2. Gunter Dufey and Ian H. Giddy, "Forecasting Exchange Rates in a
     Floating World," Euromoney, November 1975.

 3. John Norris and Michael Evans, "Beating the Futures Market in Foreign
     Exchange Rates," Euromoney, February 1976.

 4. Martin Murenbeeld, "Economic Factors for Forecasting Exchange Rate
     Changes," Columbia Journal of World Business, Fall 1975.

 5. Columbia Journal of World Business (Winter 1979): Special Issue on the
     foreign exchange market; articles by Levich and Bilson recommended.

 6. Richard M. Levich, "Analysing the Accuracy of Foreign Exchange Advisory
     Services," in Levich and Wihlborg, eds. Exchange Risk and Exposure
     (Lexington, 1980), 99-127.

5.   Exchange Risk and Exposure

2/17
     Concepts of accounting exposure; the temporal method and FASB
requirements; economic rationale for alternative approaches; recognition

of exchange gains and losses; tax effects; accounting vs. economic exposure;
how exchange rate changes affect the value of foreign operations; exchange
risk in the small and in the large; methods of risk reduction.

Case: "American Can Company" (How can ACC measure its exposure to a
peso devaluation? Should it hedge? When and how much? What
alternatives does it have? etc.)

Readings

* 1. Eiteman and Stonehill, Ch. 3.

2. Janice M. Westerfield, "How Us Multinationals Manage Currency
Risk," Fed. Res. Bank of Philadelphia Business Reviews
March/April 1980.

3. Robert Z. Aliber and Clyde P. Stickney, "Accounting Measures
of Foreign Exchange Exposure: The Long and Short of It,"
The Accounting Review, January 1975, 44-47. In Lessard, IFM.

4. E. Bruce Frederickson, "On the Measurement of Foreign Income,"
In Lessard, IFM

5. M. E. Barrett and L.L. Spero, "Accounting Determinants of
Foreign Exchange Gains and Losses, "Financial Analysts Journal,
March-April, 1975.

6. Gunter Dufey, "Corporate Finance and Exchange Rate
Variations," Financial Management, Summer 1972. In Lessard, IFM.

7. Ian H. Giddy, "Exchange Risk: Whose View? Financial Management,
Summer 1977.

8. Robert K. Ankrom, "Top Level Approach to the Foreign Exchange
Problem," Harvard Business Review, July-August 1974, 79-99
In Lessard, IFM

9. Fred Choi and Gary Meuller, Multinational Accounting and
Finance (Prentice-Hall, 1979), Ch. 3.

6. Hedging and Exchange Risk Management

2/24

Principles of exchange risk reduction: cash flow matching; balance
sheet hedging; implications of the forward rate as an unbiased predictor
of the future spot rate; the cost of hedging; spreads in the spot and forward
markets; money market and commodity market hedging; does continual forward
hedging reduce exchange risk?

Case: Review hedging approaches appropriate for American Can Co.

Reading
* 1. Eiteman and Stonehill, Ch. 4.

* 2. Steven Kohlhagen, "Evidence on the Cost of Cover in a
     Floating System," Euromoney, September 1975, 138-141.

* 3. S.R. Bradford,"Measruing the Cost of Forward Exchange
     Contracts," Euromoney, August 1974, 71-75.

  4. Guiliano Pelli, "Thoughts on the Cost of Forward Cover
     in a Floating System," Euromoney, October 1974 34-35;
     also S. R. Bradford's "Reply," Euromoney, November 1974

  5. Ian H. Giddy, "Why It Doesn't Pay to Make a Habit of
     Forward Hedging," Euromoney, December 1976, 96-100. In
     Lessard, IFM.

  6. Herbert Grubel, International Economics (Irwin, 1978)
     Ch. 12, pp. 247-259.

7. International Investment Decisions

3/3
     Definition, scope and evolution of foreign direct investment; indus-
trial organization, product life cycle, behavioral and capital market
theories; product versus geographical diversification?; financing international expansion, analyzing projected cash flows; decision criteria for
international investment; the exchange rate and inflation problems; the
repatriation problem; taxation; incorporation of risk, portfolio approach;
sensitivity analysis.

  Case: "Vick International". Perform a numerical financial analysis of the
        proposed self-medication plant in Indonesia. Organize the data,
        identify the assumptions underlying the forecasts, and consider
        alternatives to the proposal.

  Readings:
* 1. Rodriguez and Carter, Ch. 10 (Ch. 11 optional)

  2. Eiteman and Stonehill, Ch. 7

  3. Alan C. Shapiro, "Capital Budgeting for the Multinational Corporation,"
     in Lessard, IFM

  4. Donald Lessard, "Evaluating Foreign Projects," in Lessard, IFM

  5. Ian H. Giddy, "The Demise of the Product Cycle Model in International
     Business Theory," CJWB, Spring 1978, 90-97.

  6. C.P. Kindleberger, "The Theory of Direct Investment," American
     Business Abroad (New Haven: Yale University Press, 1969), Ch.1
     in Lessard, IFM.

  7. Giorgio Ragazzi, "Theories of the Determinants of Direct Foreign
     Investment," IMF Staff Papers, Vol. 20, July 1973, 471-498. In
     Lessard, IFM.

8. <u>International Financing Decisions</u>

3/10

Financing objectives of international firms and banks, link of investment to financing decisions: the cost of capital; measuring the world wide cost of capital, optional capital; optional capital structure; parent and subsidiary; range of financing alternatives: short/long, dollar/foreign currency, fixed/variable rates; and the risks. Export-import financing.

Case: "Standard Electronics International." Please help Mr. Duvalier come up with a systematic method to compare financing options in different currencies, as in the Munich loan approval request (item 3 (a) to (e)).

Readings:

* 1. Eiteman and Stonehill, Ch. 10.

2. Rodriguez and Carter, Ch. 11.

3. Ian Giddy, "The Cost of Capital in the International Firm," <u>Managerial and Decision Economics</u>, forthcoming.

4. Alan C. Shapiro, "Financial Structure and Cost of Capital in the Multinational Corporation," <u>Journal of Financial and Quantitative Analysis</u>, June 1978, 211-226.

5. Mason, Miller, and Weigel, <u>The Economics of International Business</u>, Ch. 14.

6. Sidney M. Robbins and Robert B. Stobaugh, "Financing Foreign Affiliates," <u>Financial Management</u>, Winter 1972, 56-65. In Lessard, <u>IFM</u>.

9. <u>Selected Topics in International Financial Management</u>

3/24

Bonus session, to wrap up the corporate international finance section. Review of difficult topics covered, plus discussion of one or two issues not directly addressed, such as international accounting and control, organization of the international finance function, international taxation, trade financing, project financing, acquisitions, international portfolio diversification, etc.

Possible Readings:

1. Eiteman and Stonehill, Chs. 14, 15 or 16.

2. Lessard, <u>International Financial Management</u>, Chs. 37, 38, 2, 12.

3. Sidney Robbins and Robert Stobaugh, "Multinational companies: Growth of the Financial Function," <u>Financial Executive</u> (July 1973),24-31.

4. Grover R. Castle, "Project Financing-Guidelines for the Commercial Banker," Journal of Commercial Bank Lending, April 1975, 14-30.

10. The Eurocurrency and Eurobond Markets.

3/31

The basic function of the Euromarkets; "foreign" markets; institutions and sources and uses of funds; practice: deposit markets compared; syndications; Eurobond market's role; currency and yield on Eurobonds; medium-term bank credit versus direct financing; equity financing; finance subsidiaries abroad.

Case: Munroe Coley and the Eurobond market (A)." Ask: Why Bonds? Why Euros? Why dollars? Why now?

Readings:

* 1. Eiteman and Stonehill, Ch. 9.

2. Rodriguez and Carter, Ch. 13, 14, 15.

3. Dufey and Giddy, The International Money Market, Ch. 1-5.

4. Ian Giddy, "The Blossoming of the Eurobond Market," Columbia Journal of World Business, Spring 1976.

5. Johannes Semler, "Advantages and Disadvantages of Forming Finance Subsidiaries Abroad," Euromoney, June 1974, 56-59.

6. Financing Foreign Operations, "Ways and Windows".

7. Yoon S. Park, The Eurobond Market (Praeger, 1974).

11. The Eurocurrency Market: Economics of Growth and Interest Rates

4/7

Why Eurocurrencies exist; why Eurocurrencies grow; what Eurodeposits pay what Euroloans cost; currency differences; location differences; bank differences; multiplier vs. demand/supply approach; inflationary and liquidity implications of Eurodollars.

Readings

* 1. Dufey and Giddy, The International Money Market, Chs. 2,3.

2. Jane Little, Eurodollars: The Money Market Gypsies, Ch. 2, 3.

3. Andrew Crockett, International Money (Academic Press, 1977), Ch. 10 "The Eurocurrency Market."

4. Ronald McKinnon, Money in International Exchange (Oxford, 1979), Ch. on Eurocurrency market.

12. International Banking: Strategy and Competition

4/14

Scope of international banking activities; which banks?; history; U.S. banks abroad and foreign entry to USA: theory and practice of international banking expansion; industrial organization, entry barriers and profitability; international investment banking.

Case: "Transnational Bank's African Investments." What, if anything, should TNB do about its affiliates in sub-Sahara Africa?

Readings:

* 1. Eiteman and STonehill, Ch. 13.

2. Sanford Rose, "Why They Call It Fat City," _Fortune_, February 1975.

3. Henning, Pigott and Scott, _International Financial Management_ (McGraw-Hill, 1978), Ch. 7, 8.

4. Robert Z. Aliber, "Towards a Theory of International Banking," _Federal Reserve Bank of San Francisco Review_, Spring 1976.

5. Herbert G. Grubel, "A Theory of Multinational Banking" _Banca Nazionale del Lavoro Quarterly Review_, December 1977.

6. Martin Mayer, _The Bankers_ (Ballantine paperback, 1974), Ch. 16, 17.

13. International Bank Lending

4/21

Bank lending policies, domestic, and international; limits, lines and pricing of loans; credit worthiness analysis; lending to firms, governments and banks; syndications; terms and conditions; trends and problems.

Case: Republic of Zaire."

Readings:

1. Francis A. Lees, "International Lending Strategies of Commercial Banks," _Columbia Journal of World Budiness_, Winter 1976.

2. Angelini et al., _International Lending, Risks and the Euromarkets_ (Macmillan, 1979), Ch. 1 (also 2 and 3).

3. Dufey and Giddy, _The International Money Market_, Ch. 5, part III.

4. F. John Mathis, ed., _Offshore Lending by U.S. Commercial Banks_, Various chapters.

5. T. H. Donaldson, _Lending in International Commercial Banking_, various chapters.

14. Regulation and the Future of International Banking

4/28
Monetary policy and the Eurodollar market; prudential regulation of international banking crises of the 1970's and central bank response; domestic and international allocation of credit; forms of control and their deficiencies; forms of propping-up and the moral hazard problem; innovation and the risk in the future of international banking.

Reminder: Term paper due.

Readings:

* 1. Edward J. Frydl, "The Debate Over Regulating the Eurocurrency Markets," <u>Federal Reserve Bank of New York Quarterly Review.</u>

* 2. Ian Giddy and Deborah Allen, "International Competition in Bank Regulation," <u>Banca Nazionale del Lavoro Quarterly Review</u> (No. 130 September 1979), 311-326.

3. Robert Z. Aliber, "Monetary Aspects of Offshore Markets," <u>Columbia Journal of World Business</u> (Fall 1979).

4. James W. Dean and Herbert Grubel, "Regulatory Issues and the Theory of Multinational Banking", in Frank Edwards, ed. <u>Issues in Financial Regulation</u> (McGraw-Hill, 1978).

Spring 1981   Giddy

Date	Topic	Case
Tues.		
1/20	1. Int'l finance introduction	"The Snake"
1/27	2. Int'l interest rates, exch. rates and inflation	
2/3	3. Foreign Exchange and Euro-currency trading	E&S ex. 2.3, 2.6
2/10	4. Exchange rate forecasting.	Mexican Peso
2/17	5. Exchange risk and exposure.	Amer. Can.
2/24	6. Hedging and exchange risk management.	
3/3	7. Int'l investment decisions	Vick
3/10	8. Int'l financing decisions	Std. Elec. Int'l
3/14-3/22	Mid-term recess.	
3/24	9. Selected topics or guest speaker.	
3/31	10. The Eurocurrency and Euro-bond mkts.	M. Coley (A)
4/7	11. The Eurocurrency Market: growth, int. rates.	
4/14	12. Int'l banking strategy & Compet.	TNB Afr.N.V.
4/21	13. Int'l bank lending	Zaire
4/28	14. Regulation and the Future of Int'l Banking	Term Paper Deadline

FINAL EXAM

B40.3386
International Finance

Prof. Reuven Glick
Spring 1981
407 Merrill Hall
(212) 285-6045

THE COURSE

This is an advanced course on international monetary theory and policy.
The primary focus is on the macroeconomics of balance of payments
adjustment and the international monetary system.

The course begins with a brief analysis of the foreign exchange market.
Various models of balance of payments adjustment are then developed and
integrated. Related topics, such as the J curve and exchange rate
determination, are also discussed. The last part of the course addresses
several macroeconomic policy issues including policy coordination, the choice
of exchange rate systems, the gains from common currency areas, and the
demand and supply of international liquidity.

PREREQUISITE

A previous exposure to either international economics or macroeconomics is
required for this course. Prior completion of B40.2381 (International Trade
and Finance) or B30.2331 (Macroeconomics) is sufficient. The student should
also feel reasonably comfortable with the use of graphical and mathematical
tools of economic analysis.

READINGS AND MATERIALS

Extensive readings will be assigned from the following books, which it is
recommended that students purchase at the GBA bookstore:

  R. Stern, The Balance of Payments, Chicago, Aldine, 1973.

  S. Willett, Floating Exchange Rates and International Monetary Reform,
  Washington, American Enterprise Institute, 1977.

Students may also wish to consult the following books:
  R. Dornbusch, Open Economy Macroeconomics, New York, Basic Books, 1980.

  R. Aliber, The International Money Game, New York, Basic Books, 1977,
  3rd edition.

  S. Black, Floating Exchange Rates and National Economic Policy, New
  Haven, Yale University Press, 1977.

  J. Frenkel, J. and H.G. Johnson, eds., The Monetary Approach to the
  Balance of Payments, Toronto, University of Toronto Press, 1976.

  M. Chacholiades, International Monetary Theory and Policy, New York,
  McGraw-Hill, 1978.

Further required reading assignments are listed in the course outline. A broad sample of supplementary readings on each of the topics in the outline is appended separately. A packet containing almost all of the required articles and a number of supplementary articles is available through the bookstore. These articles are indicated below by asterisks (*). Several copies of this packet as well as all the books indicated above are on reserve in the GBA library. There will be occasional xeroxed handouts during the course.

GRADING

Two examinations will be given during the term--a take-home mid-term to be given April 8 and an in-class final. The mid-term performance will count forty percent of the course grade provided it is better than the grade on the final examination. Otherwise, the mid-term grade will be disregarded.

Students who wish to improve their course grade may submit a paper which critically surveys the literature on any topic or sub-topic included in the course outline. The paper will be graded pass-fail; a passing mark will improve the final grade by one-third of a letter. A typed working outline and bibliography must be submitted by April 22; the final paper is due May 13. All papers must be typed, double spaced, and at least ten pages in length. No late papers or outlines will be accepted.

COURSE OUTLINE AND REQUIRED READINGS

I. INTRODUCTION (½ week)

International monetary issues. Plan of the course.

   Readings: Truman, E. "Balance-of-Payments Adjustment From a U.S.
             Perspective: The Lessons of the 1970's" Board of
             Governors International Finance Discussion Paper,
             June 1979, Sections I-III only (distributed in class).

II. BASIC RELATIONSHIPS IN INTERNATIONAL MACROECONOMICS (½ week)

Balance of payments accounting. National Income Accounting. Money Accounting

   Readings: Stern, R., Balance of Payments, Ch. 1.
             *Dornbusch, R., Open Economy Macroeconomics, "Some Basic
             Relations", Chapter 2.

III. FOREIGN EXCHANGE MARKET (1½ weeks)

Demand and supply for spot foreign exchange. Equilibrium, stability,
and the Marshall-Lerner condition. The spot rate under alternative monetary
standards. The forward foreign exchange market. Interest arbitrage and
the interest parity condition. Deviations from interest parity.

   Reading: Stern R., Balance of Payments, Ch. 2.
            Kubarych, R., Foreign Exchange Markets in the U.S.,
            Federal Reserve Bank of New York, 1978 (distributed in class
            skim).
            *Aliber, R., "The Interest Rate Parity Theorem: A Reinterpre-
            tation," Journal of Political Economy (Nov/Dec 1973)
            pp. 1451-59.
            *Frenkel, R., "Elasticities and Interest Parity Theory,"
            Journal of Political Economy (May 1973)
            *Frenkel and Levich, "Covered Interest Arbitrage: Unexploited
            Profits?" Journal of Political Economy, April 1975, pp.1451-

IV. BALANCE OF PAYMENTS ADJUSTMENT: THE ELASTICITY APPROACH (1 week)

Foreign exchange market and the balance of payments. Export and import
elasticity of supply and demand. Marshall-Lerner condition. J-curves.

   Reading: Stern, Balance of Payments, Ch. 5 (skim pp. 133-136).
            *Magee, S., "Currency Contracts, Pass-Through and Devaluation,"
            Brookings Papers on Economic Activity (No. 1, 1973), pp. 303-

V. BALANCE OF PAYMENTS ADJUSTMENT: THE INCOME APPROACH & THE FOREIGN TRADE
MULTIPLIER (1 week)

National income and expenditure in an open economy. Foreign trade multiplier
International transmission of income fluctuations.

   Reading: Stern, Balance of Payments, Ch. 6.

VI. BALANCE OF PAYMENTS ADJUSTMENT: THE ABSORPTION APPROACH (½ week)

Integration of absorption, income, and elasticities approaches.
Expenditure reduction and switching.

Reading: Stern, Balance of Payments, Ch. 7 (omit pp. 205-211).
*Alexander, Sidney S., Effects of a Devaluation on a
Trade Balance," IMF Staff Papers (April 1952),
pp. 263-78, reprinted in R. Caves and H. Johnson, eds.,
Readings in International Economics, Homewood, Ill.,
Irwin, 1968.

VII. BALANCE OF PAYMENTS ADJUSTMENT: INTERNATIONAL CAPITAL MOVEMENTS (1 week)

International capital movements. The transfer problem. Balance of
payments restrictions.

Reading: Stern, Balance of Payments, Ch. 8 (skim), 9 (omit pp.292-293).

VIII. BALANCE OF PAYMENTS ADJUSTMENT: MONETARY & PORTFOLIO APPROACH (3 weeks)

Role of money in balance of payments adjustment. Stock and flow equilibrium.
Determination of equilibrium income and interest rates in an open economy.
General integration of balance of payments adjustment mechanisms. Effect of
capital mobility and exchange rate regime on monetary and fiscal stabilization
policy.

Reading: Stern, Balance of Payments, Ch. 10 (pp. 312-326 only).
Herring Notes (distributed in class).
*Johnson, H. G., "The Monetary Approach to the Balance of
Payments: A Nontechnical Guide," Journal of International
Economics (August 1977), pp. 251-68.
*Kemp, D., "A Monetary View of the Balance of Payments,"
Federal Reserve Bank of St. Louis Monthly Review (July
1975).
*Magee, S., "The Empirical Evidence on the Monetary Approach
to the Balance of Payments and Exchange Rates," American
Economic Review (May 1976).

IX. MODELS OF EXCHANGE RATE DETERMINATION (1 week)

Portfolio models of balance of payments. Dynamic models of exchange rate
determination. Overshooting.

Reading: *Black, S., "The Functioning of Floating Exchange Rates in
Theory and Practice" Excerpt from Black, Floating Exchange
Rates and National Economic Policy, Ch. 1.
*Branson, W., "Exchange Rate Dynamics and Monetary Policy,"
in A. Lindbeck, ed., Inflation and Employment in Open
Economies, North Holland, 1979 (omit sections 2.2, 2.3,
2.4, 4.4).
*Dornbusch, R., "Expectations and Exchange Rate Dynamics,"
Journal of Political Economy (Dec. 1976), (skim, omit
sections III, IV, V).

X. MACROECONOMIC POLICY ISSUES: OPTIMAL POLICY MIX & ASSIGNMENT (1 week)

Conflicts between internal and external balance. Assignment of monetary and fiscal policies under conflicting goals. International coordination of policies.

   Reading: Stern, Balance of Payments, Ch. 10(pp. 305-312,326-338 only).
           Truman, E., "Balance of Payments Adjustment from a U.S.
           Perspective," Sections IV, V.

XI. MACROECONOMIC POLICY ISSUES: EXCHANGE RATE SYSTEM (1 week)

Arguments for and against fixed and flexible exchange rate regimes.

   Reading: *Artus, J. and J. Young, "Fixed and Flexible Exchange Rates:
           A Renewal of the Debate," IMF Staff Papers (December 1979).

XII. MACROECONOMIC POLICY ISSUES: OPTIMAL CURRENCY AREAS (½ week)

   Reading: *Ishiyama, Y., "Theory of Optimum Currency Areas: A Survey,"
           IMF Staff Papers (July 1975).

XIII. MACROECONOMIC POLICY ISSUES: INTERNATIONAL RESERVES & LIQUIDITY (½ week)

Composition of international reserves. Reserve adequacy. Creation of international reserves. Seigniorage problem.

   Reading: Stern, Balance of Payments, Ch. 12.

XIV. MACROECONOMIC POLICY ISSUES: THE INTERNATIONAL MONETARY SYSTEM & PLANS FOR REFORM (1 week)

History of international monetary system. Plans for reforms.

   Reading: Willett, T.D., Floating Exchange Rates and International
           Monetary Reform, Washington, American Enterprise Institute.

HARVARD UNIVERSITY
GRADUATE SCHOOL OF BUSINESS

INTERNATIONAL MANAGERIAL FINANCE
Christine R. Hekman

--Course Description and Outline--

Overview

As business opportunities become increasingly global in scope,
the distinctiveness of international markets and institutions becomes
increasingly important to corporate financial managers. This course considers
those aspects of the international environment which are unique and suggests
a conceptual framework for the financial management of the international
firm. Further, the study of foreign exchange rates motivates a deeper understanding of the effects of inflation on the financial value of the
corporation.

The cases used in the course focus on the decisions to be made by
participants in international markets. In the early part of the course we
consider the markets for foreign exchange and foreign assets with an emphasis on the risk/return characteristics of multicurrency investments. The
application of these concepts is found in the decisions which confront the
financial manager of the international firm: the management of foreign
exchange exposure, investment selection, and funding strategy. Articles and
technical notes supplement cases as the basis for class discussions.

The topics are important for bankers and corporate financial
officers who face international opportunities. It will be most useful to
students preparing for such careers.

The goal of the course is to develop skill for the recognition and
analysis of international opportunities. These skills require an understanding
of a theoretical framework for the valuation of the international firm. This
framework highlights the multicurrency dimension of firms with foreign assets and liabilities and recognizes that foreign currency cash flows have
unique characteristics of risk and return.

The application of the theory is found in the decisions which confront the financial manager: the management of foreign exchange exposure,
investment selection and financing from foreign sources. Through cases which
describe such financial opportunities, we recognize the characteristics of
product and currency markets which contribute to or detract from investment
value. We also develop techniques which simplify the analysis of such opportunities.

The distinct contribution of the course is its application of
sophisticated financial concepts to the resolution of complex international

financial decisions and to the creation of an international corporate strategy. A secondary benefit is an insight into the effect of inflation on corporate value.

Content and Organization

The theme of the course is the multicurrency dimension of the
international firm. The first half of the class sessions focus on the financial characteristics of important markets for goods, capital and foreign
exchange. The goal is to understand the ways in which rates and the volatility
of international markets affect value.

In the second half of the course, we consider the implications
of such behavior for financial decision-making and strategy formulation.
The cases also provide exposure to important international institutions and
their characteristics.

Class discussions focus around cases, notes, and readings. Both
the theory and application are developed by considering the decisions faced
by market participants.

Course requirements include a mid-term paper(1500 words) and a
final examination.

Course Outline

One session   Introduction

Six sessions   International Financial Markets

    *Understanding exchange rates as elements of a larger system.
    *Exchange rates are primarily a monetary phenomenon.
    *The important characteristics of exchange rates are trend,
     changes in trend, and variance around trend.

Nine sessions   Exchange Rates and International Firm

    *Understanding the relationship between variance in the
     economic system and variance in corporate value.
    *Interpreting the accountant's treatment of variance.
    *Analysis of opportunities to eliminate variance.
    *Organizing the exposure management function.

Eight sessions   Elements of International Investments

    *Valuing restricted cash flows.
    *The taxation of foreign earnings.
    *International transfer pricing.
    *Factoring inflation into investment value.
    *Recognizing the "currency" element of value.
    *Comparison of methods of market entry.

Five sessions   Financing International Investments

*Analysis of the costs and risks of foreign financing vehicles.
*Foreign financing as a risk reduction strategy.

One session   Strategic Considerations

*The formulation of international strategy.

One session   Review

Course Resources

Casebook (required)

Carlson, Remmers, Hekman, Eiteman, and Stonehill, International Finance: Cases and Simulation, Addison-Wesley, 1980. (IF)

Textbook (required)

Eiteman and Stonehill, Multinational Business Finance, second edition, Addison-Wesley, 1979. (MBF)

Textbook (recommended)

Robert Aliber, The International Money Game, third edition, Basic Books, 1979. (IMG)

Textbook (others)

Robert Aliber, Exchange Risk and Corporate International Finance, The MacMillan Press Ltd., 1978. (ER&CIF)

Donald R. Lessard, ed., International Financial Management, Warren Gorham & Lamont, 1979. (IFM - Lessard)

Rodrigues & Carter, International Financial Management, second edition, Prentice-Hall, Inc., 1979. (IFM)

Course Outline

I. INTRODUCTION--ONE SESSION

The readings are designed to raise students' awareness of the economic incentives for foreign investment. They suggest that such diverse elements as diversification objectives, competitive advantage, market differentiation, and taxation and regulation differences contribute to a financial manager's decision to invest across borders.

These factors are not distinctively "international;" many strictly domestic firms invest across state borders in response to similar economic incentives. However, the assigned readings suggest a distinctly international incentive for direct foreign investment--differences in foreign currency values. The rationale is that countries which serve as <u>sources</u> of international capital can issue securities which offer lower returns because their currencies are "preferred" by investors. As a result, the recent swings in investor preferences and currency strengths have caused the dramatic phenomenon of "foreigners buying up the U.S."

This explanation leaves the class with several intriguing questions which will be explored further in the course through cases, readings and class discussion.

* Can foreign exchange rate swings change the economics of finance so dramatically?

* What does this mean for the financial manager?

* Can the financial manager create value by acquiring foreign currency-denominated assets and liabilities?

* What are the risk and return characteristics of such opportunities? How can other financial instruments be used in the management of currency risk?

Reading/Case Assignment

"Howard Johnson Rounds Out
Imperial's Strong Hand"
(3-280-074)

"America Going Cheap"(3-280-075)

"German Invasion"(3-280-073)

"Why Are Multinational Firms
Mostly American?"

II. INTERNATIONAL FINANCIAL MARKETS--EXCHANGE RATES ARE DETERMINED WITHIN
     A SYSTEM--SIX SESSIONS

          Exchange rates can be described by three characteristics--level,
trend, and deviation from trend. Further, the actions of arbitrageurs,
speculators and traders drive spot exchange rates toward relationships with
interest rates, prices and forward rates. In this section, we study the
validity of these relationships by considering alternative theories of
exchange rate behavior, comparing the theories to data, and discussing the
decisions facing participants in the foreign exchange market.

     A. "The Oil Crisis and the Balance of Payments"

          The BOP accounts of Brazil, Italy, Japan and the U.K. can be used
to dissect the different responses of these economics to the 1973 Oil Crisis.
The exercise introduces students to the use of BOP data in the analysis of
macroeconomic behavior. It encourages an understanding that payments balances
and exchange rates change in response to flows of international cash in the
way that corporate equity values change as cash flows change.

Reading/Case Assignment

 The Oil Crisis and the Balance of Payments
 (9-280-069)

Introduction to Balance of Payments
Analysis(4-378-043)

Balance of Payment Concepts--
What Do They Really Mean
(8-279-027)

     B. "Brittanic International Shipping, Ltd. (C)"

          Brittanic International is evaluating alternative sources of
finance for the purchase of a tanker. As a U.K. company, its managers must
forecast the future values of the currencies denominating the loans--yen and
deutschmark. BOP data is provided which allows an analysis of the historic
cash flow of these countries. The reading assignment suggests relationships
between these flows and the behavior of such variables as interest rates,
economic growth, and unemployment. I provide unemployment statistics which are
useful in understanding the political pressures on the German, Japanese or
British governments which might encourage them to either change or defend
exchange rate parities.

Reading/Case Assignment

Brittanic International Shipping,
Ltd. (C) (9-272-025)

IMG, pp. 13-22 & 53-59

Reading/Case Assignment IIB cont.

International Financial
Statistics Yearbook 1980

Unemployment Statistics:
United Kingdom, Germany,
and Japan(8-279-046)

C. Alternative Explanation of Exchange Rate Behavior

The readings describe two basic views of balance of payments
and exchange rate behavior. The "accounting balances" view explains exchange
rate behavior as a response to the net balance of each BOP account. In order
to understand or predict the exchange rate, one must predict the individual
accounts. The "monetary" view focuses on the financial asset characteristics
of money. It emphasizes the rate of the money supply and excess money creation
in causing currency devaluation. Data is provided in the readings with which
the usefulness of each approach can be analyzed.

Reading/Case Assignment

"Oil Imports and the
Fall of the Dollar"(8-279-06)

"Reflections on the U.S.
Balance of Payments"(3-279-055)

"Trade, Capital Flows, and
Currencies"(8-279-043)

"A Monetary View of the
Balance of Payments"(8-277-011)

"The Recent U.S. Trade
Deficit"(8-279-044)

Statement by the President--
Dec. 21, 1977

D. Floating Exchange Rates--Fixed Exchange Rates

The readings describe the relationship between world trade and
the choice of monetary system. These macroeconomic relationships can be
understood at the microeconomic level by considering how different systems
affect the corporate financial officer's opportunities. This session focuses
on the variability of exchange rates around their trend.

Reading/Case Assignment

IMG, Chapter 4

Reading/Case Assignment IID cont.

"Floating Rates and World
Trade"(3-279-030)

ER&CIF, Chapter 2

    E. "The Dollar Dilemma"

        The case outlines several important elements of the economic
situation in August 1978. Flight from the dollar had reached almost epidemic
proportions while the U.S. economy was booming. The class is asked to
diagnose the problems and recommend policy solutions.

        The data show that exchange rates historically have conformed
fairly closely to relative domestic inflation levels. However, in 1978
the dollar appears substantially undervalued. One explanation is that international investors, expecting a rapid increase in U.S. inflation, are moving
out of the dollar. Supplementary tables support this by documenting a consistent underappraisal of future U.S. inflation by both domestic and international investors. The dollar is a financial asset and its price, the exchange
rate, behaves like other financial assets.

        Expectations of future U.S. inflation are supported by an
analysis of policy objectives. All of the objectives described in the case
require a continuation of expansionary macroeconomic policy.

        The case demonstrates the dilemma faced by managers of a reserve
currency country when macroeconomic policy for domestic objectives conflicts
with policy designed for external approval.

        The case concludes the section which has focused on exchange
rates and their role in the international economic system. It illustrates
through text and data the linkage between exchange rates and(both past and
expected)relative inflation. It reviews, from the policy maker's perspective, the issues raised in earlier cases. These include the costs and
benefits of defending an exchange rate against market forces, and the
elements which determine exchange rates. It demonstrates the real dilemmas
faced by the major actors in the foreign exchange market, the central banks.
Finally, it shows that movements in international capital can be swift and
strong. The resulting exchange rate swings may not be immediately reflected
in domestic prices and corporate cash flows. This variability in the
economic system can lead to real risks for the international firm.

Reading/Case Assignment

"The Dollar Dilemma"(IF, pp. 1-21)

Historical Rates of Return on
Investment(9-279-042)

Returns to the International
Investor(8-279-048)

F. "Ken and Joan Morse"

This case examines the dilemma of private investors considering speculation in foreign currency futures. Joan and Ken Morse are young, inexperienced, with very little capital. An analysis of the speculative opportunity demands that students understand the importance to the Morses of margin calls and the size of potential losses. They gain a working understanding of futures speculation which focuses on risk, timing, and required investment. They are introduced to the "snake" within which EED currencies are maintained.

The major conclusion of the case is that speculators such as the Morses, or large institutions acting on the same profit motivation, will drive the forward or futures rate to the value of the expected future spot rate.

They can also see that this determination of spot rates is perfectly consistent and can be coincidental with the equality of the forward discount and interest rate differentials.

These two relationships together with Purchasing Power Parity, developed above, describe a macroeconomic framework. The framework relates the variables which are most important to international valuation. These variables are exchange rates, interest rates and inflation rates.

Reading/Case Assignment

"Ken and Joan Morse"(9-273-018)

"Make a Killing in the Foreign
Exchange Market--or Get Killed"
(3-28-070)

"How Chicago's Foreign Exchange
Futures Market Has Worked"
(1-281-026)

"Predicting Exchange Rates:
A Return to PPP"(3-280-013)

Understanding Futures in
Foreign Exchange(pamphlet)

III. FOREIGN EXCHANGE EXPOSURE--VARIANCE IN THE EXCHANGE RATE SYSTEM CAUSES
VARIANCE IN COMPANY VALUE--EIGHT SESSIONS

The assignments encourage students to develop an understanding of foreign exchange risk--the variability in corporate value induced by variability in the exchange rate. The relevant variability is that of the dollar equivalents of the cash flow-expectations so that the relationship between exchange rates and relative prices is an important part of the equation. When exchange risk is viewed as part of the overall macroeconomic system, corporate sensitivity to exchange rate variability is mitigated by offsetting inflation changes.

As with domestic financial decisions, the students should also question the relevance of this exchange risk to financial markets. The cases progress to show that exchange risk is unsystematic, in a capital asset pricing model sense. However, in cases where total variability increases a firm's costs, there may be value in reducing the risk though hedging.

Finally, hedging alternatives(local debt, forward cover, swap loans) are evaluated. Techniques are introduced which can be used to evaluate their coasts and risk reduction characteristics.

A. Dozier Industries

In 1976, a U.S. firm had just closed its first international sales contract. The first sale, in a potentially profitable export business, was dominated in poinds sterling. Dozier had received 10% of the ₺425,000 contract and would receive the remainder, in pounds, in ninety days. The CFO had to decide whether to hedge the foreign exchange exposure. Hedging options included a forward foreign exchange sale of pounds and a pound sterling loan.

The case introduces the concept of exposure as the variability in earnings and net worth which is caused by exchange rate variability. This variability can be hedged and the cost of the hedge is the "cost" of going international. This cost should have been included in the price charged for the export, but was not. Further, the cost is equal to the lowest cost hedging option. When a hedging option is elected, the "cost" is paid with certainty. When the asset is left "unhedged," the expected cost is the same as the hedging cost, but the actual cost varies.

Because the case is fairly straightforward, the second half of class discussion focuses on the general relationships between forward discounts and interest rates. In fairly free markets, hedging is seen as "free insurance;" however, the particular opportunities available to any specific firm may make one hedging option, or no hedging relatively more attractive.

Reading/Case Assignment

Dozier Industries(IF, pp. 43-50)

Foreign Exchange Exposure
Management(9-277-183)

"Forecasting Exchange Rates
in a Floating World"(3-277-035)

MBF, pp. 91-99 & 103-116

B. American Can Company--International Business Group

By August of 1976, the Mexican peso had been pegged at a rate of MP 12.5/$ for twenty-two years. American Can Company's foreign exchange exposure manager has reason to believe that the Mexican government is about to devalue to peso. Until then, ACC's Mexican subsidiary had benefited from the lower interest costs by borrowing U.S. dollars. This strategy has left the company in a new exposed asset position. The question is--Is it time to jump ship?

The case illustrates the benefits to be gained in a fixed rate period by borrowing in the undervalued currency. However, as rates are "unstuck," such a strategy becomes quite risky. One risk is a possible reduction in net worth due to a devaluation. The class reviews the FASB-8 rules by discussing the possible size of such a reduction.

The case builds on Dozier by offering several hedging alternatives. Complications are introduced, however. One issue is that in a volatile period, cover may not be available. But even more important is the question of appropriate financial action when the manager's assessment of future exchange rates differs from the market's. The manager takes the risk of acquiring costly cover too early. Further, his/her personal costs may be quite high since most firms require high-level approval for extraordinary hedging.

Reading/Case Assignment

American Can Company--International
Business Group(IF, pp. 69-79)

MBF, pp. 91-99 & 120-138

Accounting for Foreign Operations
(9-177-046)

A Note on Foreign Currency
Accounting Issues--1976(9-176-226)

"Exchange Risk and Yield
Differentials"(ER&CIF, Chapter 3)

FASB Statement No. 8(3-281-031)

C. Continental Group--SLW

Continental's earnings have been buffeted by FASB-8 and exchange rate swings. The treasurer is evaluating several methods of eliminating exposure in the German subsidiary. Each method is seen to impose costs on the company and the students must decide whether it is worth incurring these to avoid variability in earnings induced by exchange rate changes. Data on the performance of the company's stack is provided and gives little evidence that financial markets are being affected by the variability.

The case provides data which can be used to introduce the concept of economic exposure, i.e. the sensitivity of the company's revenues, costs, and investment values to DM revaluation. It also introduces equity market response into consideration.

Reading/Case Assignment

The Continental Group, Inc.--SLW
(9-278-147)

"FASB-8: What Has It Done for
Us"(3-279-065)

"FASB No. 8 and the Decision
Makers"(3-281-030)

MBF, pp. 146 & 147

D. FASB-8 and Foreign Currency Translation

The case is really a collection of articles analyzing the effects of FASB-8 and its relevance as a descriptor of reality. It illustrates the effects of the rules on two companies: a small real estate developer investing in Canada, and Exxon. These problems highlight those aspects of the accounting rules which cause accounting exposure to diverge from economic reality. In exploring these differences the students must consider the specific measurement of economic exposure. The case suggests that FASB-8 has caused or will cause managers in these companies to make improper divestiture or financing decisions.

Though earlier cases illustrated that accounting exposure is, for many companies, irrelevant, students see the importance of the accounting treatment when it affects management behavior. Further, the class senses that "real" exposure constitutes real risk which may be worthwhile hedging. It is difficult and costly, however, to quantify real exposure using the FASB-8 accounting presentation.

Several alternative accounting treatments are analyzed and compared to the standards implicit in the above concerns. The conclusion is that three types of information are missing from the current statements:

1) Financial data disaggregated by currency.
2) Currency and maturities of long-term debt.
3) Current costs of assets--at least inventory.

A mandate of current cost accounting and amortization of losses and gains on long-term debt essentially increase disclosure and provides most of items 2) and 3).

The case can be used to focus on real exposure through a series of questions.

Specifically, what is "real" exposure? How do you measure it? How much of the required data is available from public financial statements? What required information is missing?

Reading/Case Assignment

FASB-8 and Foreign Currency
Translation(IF, pp. 33-42)

"Accounting Measures of Foreign
Exchange Exposure: the Long and
Short of It"(IFM--Lessard)

"On Revising FASB-8--Use
a Band-Aid or Major Surgery?"
(80339)

E. Machine Outil S.A.

The case introduces a risk of hedging in the forward market which is often overlooked. This risk is that the hedged case flow does not mature at the expected date or in the expected amount.

This Swiss subsidiary of U.S. parent corporation is contemplating the exchange risk involved in a bid they will submit to a U.S.S.R. firm. Some, all, or none of the $60 million will be accepted. Since the Swiss firm's costs are in SFr and the customer will only agree to terms denominated in dollars, acceptance of the bid would create an asset exposure in dollars. Any amount from none to all of this exposure may be covered for any maturities.

The two conclusions are "rules of thumb" for forward cover:

1) To minimize the variance of the outcomes, hedge the expected exposure--the mean of the possible bid acceptance amounts;

2) Variance is minimized when the forward contracts match the expected maturities of the cash flows.

Earlier cases developed a superficial but powerful characterization of forward contracts(in efficient markets) as "free insurance." This case illustrates that even when "free," such contracts may not be full-coverage "insurance." When the maturities or amounts of the underlying exposure change, the firm becomes susceptible to foreign changes.

The case introduces the notion of hedging by pricing at the expected future exchange rate.

Last, the relationships between exchange risk, relative in-flation, and competitive postion are reviewed and extended. This provides a good deal of closure to this section on exchange risk.

Reading/Case Assignment

Machine Outil, S.A.(distributed)

F. Interchemical Group (B)

A task force of financial specialists in a German multinational chemical firm has recommended a centralized reporting, cash management, and foreign exchange exposure system. Traditionally, operating and financial decisions have been totally decentralized with managers in foreign countries exercising almost total control. However, the combination of DM strength and exchange rate volatility, has combined to reduce translated foreign profits and undermine their predictability. As a result, morale was at an all-time low. In addition, it was felt that the German stock market had reacted unfavorably to the consequences of the foreign exchange exposure.

The issue in the case is that a large firm with exposures in several currencies is in a very different position from small firms exposed to the fluctuations of only single currency. Since currency risks are diversifiable, the system as a whole may experience little, if any, net exposure. A firm which never hedges may be no more variable than a firm which hedges each exposure.

In this case, the large organizational costs of centralizing a decentralized system can be avoided, but correct behavior encouraged. Simply evaluate the decentralized decision makers independent of exchange rate changes.

The case concludes the section on exposure management. The discussion of the task force report reinforces and reviews earlier concepts on appropriate hedging behavior. These concepts are challenged and modified when the exchange rates relevant to a single firm are less that perfectly correlated.

Reading/Case Assignment

Interchemical Group(9-277-616)

MBF, pp. 99-102

G. Dana Pharmaceutical Company

The financial officer of Dana is considering the wisdom of increasing the company's net working capital investment in its Mexican subsidiary. The case provides data which shows that the investment is long-term and highly exposed to exchange rate changes. Only short-term hedges are available--forward cover and a currency swap. The costs of these are different and the lowest cost hedge should be chosen if the manager decides to hedge. However, hedging has some costs which will accumulate as the hedges are rolled over throughout the investment's maturity. Further, such rollovers dramatically reduce the hedge's risk reduction characteristics.

This complex case was used as the basis for review. It raises the issues of currency risk and hedging cost and requires the use of the concepts raised in the first half of the course.

Reading/Case Assignment

Dana Pharmaceutical(9-2-7-073)

IV. FOREIGN INVESTMENTS AND THEIR VALUES

The section begins with an introduction to two important environmental considerations--taxation of foreign earnings and unrepatriatable cash.

Following these, the cases build on the earlier understanding of currency risk and the relationship between exchange rates and inflation rates. The first topic exchange risk, together with international diversification, determine the appropriate discount rate for the evaluation of foreign projects. The second factor, exchange rates and inflation, is important in determining the cash flows and matching the currency of their denomination to the currency used for the discount rate. The importance of correct evaluation is shown in several of the later cases.

At the end of the section, several methods of market entry are introduced and their effect on investment and company value considered. A broad case describing investment strategy and a case bridging to the financing section concludes this topic.

A. Macomber Operation

Macomber has the opportunity to exploit the low-wage, low-tax environment of Puerto Rico. The tax considerations come, however, only when investment earnings are retained for 10 years in Puerto Rico where they can be reinvested only at a very low rate. The value of this opportunity must be determined.

The case illustrates a common problem--non-repatriatable cash. In fact, foreign earnings of U.S. firms are not taxed in the U.S. until funds are repatriated. The required analysis is, therefore, a basic tool of international financial management.

The case also introduces students to these tax considerations and requires them to consider the dynamic effects of their decision on the reinvestment rate and the IRS's willingness to continue the tax loophole. This last consideration affects the risk of the investment.

Reading/Case Assignment

Macomber Corporation(9-176-087)

MBF, pp. 577-595

For next 6 classes:
MBF, Chapters 7, 8 & 10

B. Taxation of Americans Working Overseas

This case uses the context of a tax policy decision to demonstrate the dual and competing characteristics of tax systems. Taxation either promotes fairness by taxing on the basis of citizenship or encourages economic efficiency by taxing on the basis of production location. In order to consider the relative effects of one new international tax law on these conflicting goals, students much examine the probable effects of the law on international firms. Any detrimental effect on U.S. production capacity is compared to the positive aspect of increased tax revenues.

The tax policy under discussion is the taxation of U.S. citizens employed abroad. Before the 1976 tax reform their income had been largely sheltered from U.S. taxation. However, the new law dramatically increased their tax liability. Those who advocated equity in taxation argued that each U.S. citizen should pay his/her share. Opponents of the new tax countered that U.S. competitive advantage in international markets would be destroyed.

The case provides data to examine these claims and to consider the magnitudes of the "costs" and "benefits" of continued subsidization of citizens abroad.This determination follows from a comparison between the characteristics of U.S. firms abroad and the characteristics of firms most likely hurt by the new law.

As a by-product of this discussion, students confront issues of wider relevance than taxation regulation. They conclude that most U.S. firms selling abroad offer differentiated or technologically advanced products. It seems the U.S. economy generates firms with a special type of international competitive advantage.

This broader focus serves as a transition to the subsequent cases on foreign direct investment. It also suggests an important dimension to be considered in strategic investment planning.

Reading/Case Assignment

Taxation of Americans Working
Overseas(IF, pp. 327-344)

IMG, pp. 202-205 & 213-215

MBF, Chapter 16

C. Brooke Bond Liebig Ltd. (A)

The case outlines this British meat and tea company's approach to international investment planning. The company weighed international risks and returns to arrive at a target for the geographic spread of investments. Students discuss the usefulness of the various measures of risk used by the company. They also question an approach which allocates investments based primarily on geography. They formulate an alternative approach which weights the "pull" of marketing opportunities more strongly.

This case, which emphasizes strategic considerations, encourages a review of the basic concepts important for international investment and requires that these concepts be considered within a perspective.

Reading/Case Assignment

Brooke Bond Liebig Ltd. (A)
(9-275-092)

D. Alcan Aluminum (B)

The case presents one company's method for evaluating the expansion of foreign capacity for processing an intermediate product. The analysis affords an opportunity to consider basic techniques of international capital budgeting. These include recognition of exchange rate-price level relationships as well as accounting for system synergies.

Reading/Case Assignment

Alcan Aluminum (B)(1-281-034)

MBF, Chapter 7 & Appendix

Alcan Aluminum (A)(1-281-033)

IFM--Lessard, "Evaluating Foreign
Products: An Adjusted Present
Value Approach"(1-281-033)

E. Romar Industries

This examines international diversification from an investment management point of view. It is useful in appraising the appropriate discount rate for use in international capital budgeting.

Reading/Case Assignment

Romar Industries

"A New Route to Higher
Returns and Lower Risks"
(1-277-702)

F. Vick International--Latin America/Far East

The division's general manager must decide whether to move ahead with a direct investment in Indonesia. The usual numerical analysis does not support a positive decision, but the manager's senses tell him to move ahead. By carefully considering the nature of the product and the company, it becomes clear that one must "look through" the numbers to the people and policies which make the investment. This process suggests that the cash flows may be quite conservative. In addition, the analysis assumed implicitly that the exchange rate and Indonesian inflation would track each other. When the actual inflation, exchange rate and value results are progressively put before the class, they see the full value of the investment. As it turned out, 25% of the unexpected success of the investment came through the rapid Indonesion inflation--and the absence of a compensating rupiah devaluation.

The case does four things. It demonstrates that numerical analysis is only a tool and that success depends on understanding the numbers. Second, it demonstrates forcefully the importance of currency considerations. It forces a review of the techniques of analysis and consideration of the implicit assumptions on which such analysis is based. Finally, it begins a series of four cases in which market entry techniques are important.

Reading/Case Assignment

Vick International--Latin America/
Far East (IF, pp. 98-113)

V. FINANCING FOREIGN OPERATIONS--FIVE SESSIONS

This concluding section in many ways ties together the various themes raised in the preceding four sections. The costs of foreign currency finance are evaluated and their effect on the overall risk of the international company determined. The balance between cost and risk must be considered. Finally, international investment and international financing considerations are considered as part of an overall strategy.

A. The Borrowing Strategy of the World Bank

The case presents the data and analytical approach used by the World Bank Staff to evaluate the success of its efforts to "pick currencies" for debt denomination. The data can be used to evaluate the Bank's success for a single time period. Students can also recommend an expansion of the analytical method with which to evaluate the consistency of success.

Reading/Case Assignment

The Borrowing Strategy of
the World Bank (0-281-058)

"Once the World Bank Starts to
Borrow in Sterling Expect Others
to Follow"

"World Bank Plans No
Dollar Bond Issue"

B. International Metals, Ltd.

A British metal processing firm's managing director is faced with several alternative sources of finance for the company's ₤20 million require-mens. The choices differ by currency denomination and interest cost and included several currency cocktails, mixed currency financing.

The case is used to introduce or reinforce the concept that the cost of foreign currency debt includes two elements:

1) the interest rate and 2) the expected revaluation of the foreign currency. It also exposes students to currency cocktails such as SDR bonds and requires that they consider their pricing. This discussion reinforces the concept of currency diversification and its availability through combinations of alternative debt instruments.

These concepts are important to the course in that they provide another perspective on the risk characteristics of foreign currency financing and their effect on the currency risk of the firm.

Reading/Case Assignment

International Metals, Ltd.
(1-281-035)

MBF, pp. 330-332 & 354-361

IFM, pp. 572-574

C. Munroe Coley (A) and (B)

The financial manager of a medium-sized firm is considering whether or not to move ahead with a Eurodollar bond issue designed to finance international growth. The (A) case is set in November-December 1978 when the Euromarkets were in disarray. The puzzle is whether a lower-rated company should enter this market, at a higher cost initially, in order to gain access to a periodically cheaper source of funds. The case includes data on the growth of this market, the changing nature of its borrowers and its cyclicality.

The (B) case describes the decision to postpone the earlier offering and questions the wisdom of an issue in the spring of 1979. At this time, many firms were lining up to enter the Eurobond market. A managing director of Morgan Stanley and director of international department, John Hyland, provided data on the spreads between the Euro and U.S. bond markets. After a short class discussion of the case, he spoke and answered questions about the Eurobond and Eurodollar markets.

Reading/Case Assignment

Munroe Coley and the Eurobond
Market (A & B) (IF, pp. 132-154)

MBF, pp. 308-330

"Eurobonds--Recent Buying Panic
Causes Rise in Prices of Five
to 10 Points"(3-281-032)

D. Tektronix, Inc.

The A.V.P. finance must design a financial plan for the U.S. electronics firm's U.K. subsidiary. The firm's corporate objectives include maximization of earnings, minimization of risk and maintenance of the "good citizen" image in each country in which it operates. The immediate challenge is that the directors wish to refund $23 million in short-term and to raise an additional $7--17 million in long-term debt. The financial plan for the U.K. subsidiary must reflect these goals. It must also be founded on basic principles so that the plan will serve as a guide for other foreign subsidiaries

The financial planning problem is solved in four steps. First, the corporate leverage objective and its implications for financing are established. Second, this objective, together with an understanding regarding the capitalization norms in the U.K., recommends a level of debt for the U.S. subsidiary. Third, the appropriate currency denomination of this debt is determined by estimating alternative costs of debt and considering the effects on risk or exposure of foreign currency debt. The case demonstrates that any cost savings will represent the price they are paying for this decision. Lastly, the plan must provide for the execution of the above recommendations. The appropriate level and currency structure of the subsidiary's debt capital can be achieved through repayment of intercompany loans, collection of intercompany receivables, transfer pricing and dividend policy.

The case is an excellent vehicle for review because the solution to the problems it raises must recognize the interrelationships between 1) the parent corporation and the foreign subsidiary and 2) the financial functions of investment, financing and exposure management. These interrelationships are major distinguishing features of international financial management.

Reading/Case Assignment

Tektronix, Inc.(IF, pp. 200-215)

MBF, pp. 361-373

E. George Kent/Brown Boveri

The case considers the opportunities and problems that arise when nationality (not currency) of capital supply is at issue. It also encourages students to consider the process dynamics for a situation where one is dealing in private markets instead of public. Finally, the presence of the U.K. government in the case dynamics focuses attention on the characteristics of negotiation when one party to a deal is not a profit maximizer.

Reading/Case Assignment

George Kent/Brown Boveri--
Anatomy of a Marriage (A)
(9-277-017)

COURSE OUTLINE AND READING LIST

REQUIRED TEXTS: Leland B. Yeager, International Monetary Relations:
Theory, History and Policy, 2nd edition (N.Y.;
Harper & Row, 1976).
Richard E. Caves and Donald W. Jones, World Trade and
Payments, 2nd edition (Boston: Little, Brown & Co.,197

Recommended Purchases for those who are interested in possibly
majoring in or working in the area of international finance.
(I have knowingly by-passed the hard-core (real trade theory)
works. If interested in this area, please contact me.

R.N. Cooper, International Finance (paperback),
(Penguin: Baltimore, 1969).

R.M. Stern, The Balance of Payments (Aldine, Press:
Chicago, 1973). This is an excellent book. I am
going to 'steal' a lot of material from it. I will
let you know the areas from which I have stolen.

R.A. Mundell, International Economics, Macmillan.

R.E.Caves and H.G. Johnson, eds., AEA Readings in
International Economics.

L.H. Officer and T.D.Willett, eds., The International
Monetary System (Paperback).

E.E. Leamer and R.H. Stern, Quantitative International
Economics.

Important Reference Works

T. Scitovsky, Money and the Balance of Payments
J.E. Meade, Vol. I., The Balance of Payments
Jacob Viner, Studies in the Theory of International
Trade
H.G. Grubel, ed., World Monetary Reform: Plans and
Issues
R.A. Mundell and A.Swoboda, Monetary Problems of the
International Economy.
L.A. Metzler & H.S. Ellis, eds., A.E.A. Readings in
the Theory of International Trade
C. Haberler, Money in the International Economy,
Harvard University Press, 1965 (pamphlet)
George N. Halm, ed., Approaches to Greater Flexibility
of Exchange Rates: The Burgenstock Papers
International Monetary Funds, International Reserves:
Needs and Availability
R.A. Mundell, Monetary Theory, Goodyear Pub. Co.
J.A. Frenkel and H.G. Johnson, eds., The Monetary
Approach to the Balance of Payments, George Allen
& Unwin Ltd., London, 1976.

Abbreviations for Journals

Journal of Political Economy: J.P.E.
American Economic Review: A.E.R.
Journal of Money, Credit and Banking: J.M.C.B.
Canadian Journal of Economics: C.J.E.
Quarterly Journal of Economics: Q.J.E.
Journal of International Economics: J.I.E.

I. A "shallow" discussion by me regarding "real" trade theory.

A. Yeager, Ch. 1: Caves & Jones, Chs. 1-10.

I will draw on these chapters in our discussion plus common
published works in the literature. Sources other than Yeager
and Cave & Jones will be specified as we go along. I do not
feel guilty about having a shallow discussion here as MBA
students do not require an in-depth treatment of this area.

A. Yeager, Ch. 2; Caves & Jones, Ch. 17.

II. Balance of Payments Concepts and Measurement

A. Yeager, Ch. 3
B. Stern, Ch. 3
C. C.P. Kindleberger, "Measuring Equilibrium in the Balance of
           Payments", Journal of Political Economy (Nov/Dec.,1969)
           873-91.
D. D.T. Devlin, "The U.S.Balance of Payments: Revised Presentation"
           Survey of Current Business June, 1971.
E. H.G. Johnson,"The Balance of Payments"
F. D. Kemp, "Balance of Payments Concepts--What Do They Really
           Mean?" Federal Reserve Bank of St. Louis Review
           (July, 1975).

III. The Foreign Exchange Market

A. Yeager, Ch. 2; Cave & Jones, Ch. 17
B. L.H. Officer and T.D. Willett, "The Covered-Arbitrage Schedule:
           A Critical Survey of Recent Developments" Journal of
           Money, Credit and Banking (May, 1970).
C. H.G. Grubel, Forward Exchange, Speculation and the International
           Flow of Capital (Stanford University Press, 1966).
D. T.D. Willett, "The Eurodollar Market, Speculation and Foreign
           Exchange" (J.M.C.B. August, 1972)
E. A.R. Holmes & R.E. Schott, The New York Foreign Exchange Market

IV. Balance of Payments Adjustment

A. Yeager, Chs. 4-14.
B. Stern, Chs. 3-7.
C. Cooper, pp. 25-37, pp. 237-55.
D. R.A. Mundell, "The International Disequilibrium System" Ch.15
           R.A. Mundell, International Economics (Macmillan:
           New York, 1963).

E.   Anne O. Krueger, "Balance of Payments Theory" Journal of Economic Literature (March, 1969), 1-26.

F.   R. Harrod, Money (St. Martin's: London) Ch. 9.

G.   T.D. Willett and E. Tower, "The Welfare Economics of International Adjustment" Journal of Finance (May 1971) 287-302.

H.   D. Wrightsman, "IS,LM and External Equilibrium: A Graphical Analysis," American Economic Review (March 1970) 203-208.

I.   F. Hirsch, "The Politics of World Money" The Economist Aug. 5, 1972. 55-68.

J.   M. Friedman, "The Case for Flexible Exchange Rates" from M. Friedman, Essays in Positive Economics (University of Chicago Press: Chicago, 1953) 157-203.

K.   R.A. Mundell, "The Monetary Dynamics of International Adjustme under Fixed and Flexible Exchange Rates," Ch. 11 in R.A. Mundell International Economics (Macmillan: New York, 1968).

L.   H.G. Johnson "Towards a General Theory of the Balance of Payments" reading no. 23 in AEA Readings in International Economics (eds. R.E. Caves, H.G. Johnson) (Irwin: Homewood, Ill. 1968).

M.   L. Metzler, "The Process of International Adjustment under Conditions of Full Employment: A Keynesian View"

V.   Monetary and Fiscal Policies for Internal and External Balance

A.   Stern, Ch. 10

B.   R.A. Mundell, "The Appropriate Use of Monetary and Fiscal Policy under Fixed Exchange Rates" in R.S. Thorn, Monetary Theory and Policy 655-62.

C.   W.H. Branson, "Monetary Policy and the New View of International Capital Movements" Brookings Papers on Economic Activity Vol. 2 (1970) pp. 235-70.

D.   T.D. Willett and F. Forte, "Interest Rate Policy and External Balance" Quarterly Journal of Economics (May 1969) 242-62.

VI.   The International Monetary System

A.   Stern, Ch. 12

B.   H.G. Johnson "Theoretical Problems..." in Cooper pp. 304-34.

C.   Officer and Willett, pp. 1-32, 33-52, 139-150, 168-176, 337-357.

D.   H.G. Grubel, "The Demand for International Reserves: A Critical Review of the Literature" Journal of Economic Literature (Dec. 1971) 1148-66.

E.   J.H. Williamson, "International Liquidity" The Economic Journal (Sept. 1973) 685-746.

F.   R.I. McKinnon, Private and Official International Money: The Case for the Dollar, Princeton Essays no. 74.

G.   Confidence Problems with the U.S. dollar as international money.

    1. P.B. Kenen, "International Liquidity and the Balance of Payments of a Reserve-Currency Country" Q.J.E. (Nov.1960)) 572-86.

      2. L.H. Officer and T.D. Willett, "Reserve-Asset
         Preferences and the Confidence Problem in the Crisis
         Zone" Q.J.E. (Nov. 1969) 688-95.
      3. J.H. Makin "Swaps and Roosa Bonds as an Index of the
         Cost of Cooperation in the 'Crisis Zone'", Q.J.E.
         May 1971) 349-46.
      4. J.H. Makin "On the Success of the Reserve Currency
         System in the Crisis Zone" J.I.E. (May 1972) 77-86.

  H. Special Drawing Rights
      1. F. Machlup, Remaking the International Monetary System:
         The Rio Agreement and Beyond (John Hopkins: Baltimore,
         1968).
      2. J.H. Makin,"The Problem of Coexistence of SDRs and
         a Reserve Currency" J.M.C.B. (August 1972) 509-28.

  I. Euro-dollars:
      1. A. K. Swoboda, The Euro-dollar Market: An Interpretation
         Princeton Essays no. 64.
      2. F. Klopstock, The Euro-dollar Market: Some First
         Principles" Morgan Guaranty Survey, October 1969
         pp. 4-14.
      3. E. Clendenning, "Euro-dollars and Credit Creation",
         International Currency Review (Mar./Apr.1971) 12-19.
      4. F. Machlup,"Euro-dollar creation: A Mystery Story"
         Princeton Reprints in International Finance, No.16,
         December 1970.
      5. J.H. Makin, "Demand and Supply Functions for Stocks
         of Euro-dollar Deposits: An Empirical Study" Review
         of Economics and Statistics (November 1972) 381-391.
      6. J.H. Makin, "Identifying a Reserve Base for the Euro-
         dollar System" Journal of Finance (June 1973).

  J. Optimum Currency Areas
      1. R.A. Mundell, "A Theory of Optimum Currency Areas"
         A.E.R. (November 1961) 509-16.
      2. R. McKinnon in Cooper pp. 223-34
  K. Recent Changes in the International Monetary System
      1. J.H. Makin, "Capital Flows and Exchange-Rate Flexib-
         ility in the Post-Bretton Woods Era" Essays in
         International Finance, No. 193, February 1974,
         Princeton University, International Finance Section.
      2. Marina V.N. Whitman, "The Current and Future Role of
         the Dollar: How much Symmetry?" Brookings Papers on
         Economic Activity, 3, 1974.

VII. International Capital Flows

  A. W.H. Branson, "Monetary Policy and the New View of Inter-
         national Capital Movements" Brookings Papers on
         Economic Activity Vol.2 (1970) 235-71.
  B. Stern, Chs. 8,9.
  C. T.D. Willett and F. Forte "Interest Rate Policy and External
         Balance," Q.J.E. (May 1969) 242-62.

VIII. Growth and the Balance of Payments

    A.   Stern Ch. 11
    B.   Ch. 9 in R.A. Mundell, _International Economics_ (Macmillan: New York, 1968).

IX.   History & Policy

    A.   Yeager, Chs. 15-32.

SUPPLEMENT A (WITH DUPLICATION) TO READING LIST

(*)   Indicates recommended reading

I.   The Foreign Exchange Market

    1.   *Stern, Ch. 2.

    2.   *L.H. Officer and T.D. Willett, "The Covered-Arbitrage
        Schedule: A Critical Survey of Recent Developments,"
        JMCB (May 1970).

    3.   *T.D. Willet, "The Eurodollar Market, Speculation and
        Forward Exchange," JMCB (Aug. 1972).

    4.   *H.G. Grubel, Forward Exchange, Speculation and the Inter-
        national Flow of Capital (Stanford U. Press, 1966),
        pp. 1-56.

    5.   A.R. Holmes and F.H. Schott, The New York Foreign Exchange
        Market.

II.   Balance of Payments Adjustment

    1.   *Stern, Chs. 3-7.

    2.   Cooper, pp. 25-37, pp. 237-55.

    3.   *R.A. Mundell, "The International Disequilibrium System,"
        Ch.15 in R.A. Mundell, International Economics
        (Macmillan: N.Y., 1968).

    4.   *Anne O. Krueger, "Balance of Payments Theory," Journal of
        Economic Literature (March 1969), 1-26.

    5.   R.Harrod, Money (St. Martin's: London), Ch. 9.

    6.   T.D. Willett and E. Tower, "The Welfare Economics of Inter-
        national Adjustment," Journal of Finance (May 1971),
        pp. 287-302.

    7.   *D. Wrightsman, "IS,LM and External Equilibrium: A Graphical
        Analysis," American Economic Review (March 1970),
        pp. 203-208.

    8.   F. Hirsch, "The Politics of World Money," The Economist,
        Aug.5, 1972, pp. 55-68.

    9.   *M. Friedman, "The Case for Flexible Exchange Rates," from
        M. Friedman, Essays in Positive Economics (U.of Chicago
        Press: Chicago, 1953), pp. 157-203.

   10.   *R.A. Mundell, "The Monetary Dynamics of International
        Adjustment under Fixed and Flexible Exchange Rates,"
        Ch. 11 in R.A. Mundell International Economics
        (Macmillan: N.Y.,1968).

11. *H.G. Johnson "Towards a General Theory of the Balance of Payments," reading no.23 in AEA Readings in <u>International Economics</u> (eds. R.E.Caves and H.G.Johnson.)

III. Monetary and Fiscal Policies for Internal and External Balance

1. *Stern, Ch. 10.

2. *R.A. Mundell, "The Appropriate Use of Monetary and Fiscal Policy Under Fixed Exchange Rates," in R.S. Thorn, <u>Monetary Theory and Policy</u>, pp. 655-662.

3. W.H. Branson, "Monetary Policy and the New View of International Capital Movements," <u>Brookings Papers on Economic Activity</u>, VI. 2 (1970), pp. 235-70.

4. T.D. Willett and F. Forte, "Interest Rate Policy and External Balance," <u>Quarterly Journal of Economics</u> (May 1969), pp. 242-262.

5. S.W. Arndt, "Policy Choices in an Open Economy: Some Dynamic Considerations," <u>J.P.E.</u> (July/August 1972), pp. 916-935.

6. * B.B. Aghelvi and G.H. Borts, "The Stability and Equilibrium of the Balance of Payments Under a Fixed Exchange Rate," <u>J.I.E.</u> (Feb.1973), pp. 1-20.

7. Two Economy Models:

   a. *Mundell (No.2), Ch. 18 (Appendix especially).

   b. *R.N. Cooper, "Macroeconomic Policy Adjustment in Interdependent Economies," <u>Q.J.E.</u> (Feb.1969), pp. 1-24.

   c. M.C. Kemp, "Monetary and Fiscal Policy Under Alternative Assumptions About International Capital Mobility," <u>Economic Record</u> (Dec. 1966), pp. 598-605.

   d. Roper, Don E., "Macroeconomic Policies and the Distribution of the World Money Supply," <u>Q.J.E.</u>, Vol. LXXXV, No. 1 (Feb.1971), pp. 119-146.

8. Important Articles on Various Aspects of Open Economy Adjustment

   a. *S.C. Tsiang, "The Role of Money in Trade-Balance Stability: Synthesis of the Elasticity and Absorption Approaches," <u>American Economic Review</u> (1961), pp. 912-936. (Also in Cooper, pp. 135-164.)

   b. *S.C. Tsiang, "Capital Flows, Internal and External Balance," <u>The Quarterly Journal of Economics</u> (May 1975), pp. 195-214.

   c. P.J. Kouri and M.G. Porter, "International Capital Flows and Portfolio Equilibrium," <u>J.P.E.</u> (May/June 1974), pp. 443-468.

   d. *S.J. Turnovsky and A. Kaspura, "An Analysis of Imported Inflation in a Short-Run Macroeconomic Model," <u>Canadian Journal of Economics</u> (Aug.1974), pp. 355-378.

e. D.L. Brite and J.D.Richardson, "Some Disequilibrium Dynamics of Exchange Rate Changes," J.I.E. (Feb.1975), pp. 1-14.

f. *R. Dornbusch, "Exchange Rate Expectations and Monetary Policy," J.I.E. (Aug.1976), pp. 231-244.

g. J. Niehaus, "Some Doubts About the Efficacy of Monetary Policy Under Flexible Exchange Rates," J.I.E. (Aug.1975), pp. 275-282.

h. M. Connolly and D. Taylor, "Adjustments to Devaluation with Money and Nontraded Goods," J.I.E. (Aug.1976), pp. 289-298.

i. J.H. Makin, "A General Model for Analysis of Open Economies," mimeo.

9. Goal-Instrument: Methodological Literature

a. *H. Theil, "Linear Decision Rules for Macrodynamic Policy Problems," in B.Hickman(ed.), Quantitative Planning of Economic Policy (Wash.,D.C.: Brookings Institution,1965), pp. 18-42.

b. J.H. Wood, "A Model of Federal Reserve Behavior," in G. Horwich (ed.), Monetary Process and Policy: A Symposium (Irwin, 1967), pp. 135-166. (See appendix especially)

c. J.D. Patrick, "Establishing Convergent Decentralized Policy Assignment," J.I.E. (Feb.1973), pp.37-52.

d. P. Fortin, "Can Economic Policy Pair Instruments and Targets? (Or Should It?)," Canadian Journal of Economics (Nov. 1974), pp. 558-577.

e. W. Brainard, "Uncertainty and the Effectiveness of Policy," American Economic Review (May 1967), pp. 411-425

f. J.H. Makin, "Constraints on Formulation of Models for Measuring Revealed Preferences of Policy-Makers," KYKLOS, 1977.

IV. The Monetary Approach to the Balance of Payments and Forerunners

1. Frenkel and Johnson, entire.

2. *H.G. Johnson, "Money and the Balance of Payments," Banca Nazionale Del Lavoro Quarterly Review (March 1976), pp.3-18.

3. H.G. Johnson, "Towards a General Theory of the Balance of Payments," reading no. 23 in AEA Readings in International Economics, eds., R.E. Caves and H.G. Johnson (Irwin: Homewood, Ill., 1968).

4. F.H. Hahn, "The Balance of Payments in a Monetary Economy," Review of Economic Studies 26 (1959), pp. 110-125.

5. M.C. Kemp, "The Rate of Exchange, the Terms of Trade and the Balance of Payments in Fully Employed Economies," International Economic Review (Sept.1962), pp. 314-327.

6. I.F. Pearce, "The Problem of the Balance of Payments," _International Economic Review_ (Jan. 1961), pp. 1-28.

7. T. Negishi, "Approaches to the Analysis of Devaluation," _International Economic Review_ (1968), pp. 218-227.

8. *R. Dornbusch, "Currency Depreciation, Hoarding and Relative Prices," _J.I.E._ (July/Aug. 1973), pp. 893-915.

9. R. Dornbusch, "Devaluation, Money and Nontraded Goods," _American Economic Review_ (Dec.1973), pp. 871-880.

10. *M. Mussa, "A Monetary Approach to Balance of Payments Analysis," _JMCB_ (Aug.1974), pp. 333-351.

11. S. Alexander, "Effects of a Devaluation on the Trade Balance," _IMF Staff Papers_ (April 1952), pp. 263-278.

12. H.G. Grubel, Domestic Origins of the Monetary Approach to the Balance of Payments," _Princeton Essays in International Finance_, No. 117, June 1976.

13. M.C. Kemp, "The Balance of Payments and the Terms of Trade in Relation to Financial Controls," _Review of Economic Studies_ (Jan. 1970), pp. 25-31.

V. The International Monetary System: Background and Transition

1. Background

   a. *Stern, Ch. 12.

   b. *H.G. Johnson, "Theoretical Problems...", in Cooper, pp. 304-34.

   c. H.G. Grubel, "The Demand for International Reserves: A Critical Review of the Literature," _Journal of Economic Literature_ (Dec.1971), pp. 1148-1166.

   d. J.H. Williamson, "International Liquidity," _The Economic Journal_ (Sept. 1973), pp. 685-746.

   e. R.I. McKinnon, _Private and Official International Money: The Case for the Dollar_, Princeton Essays No. 74.

   f. Mundell, No. 16, Part II.

   g. H.G. Johnson, No. 4, pp. 304-336.

   h. H.G. Grubel, ed., _World Monetary Reform_, Chs. 1,2,5. No.5, entire.

   i. F. Machlup, _Remaking the International Monetary System: The Rio Agreement and Beyond_, No.11, pp. 21-40 and pp. 393-400.

   j. R.A. Mundell, "Toward A Better International Monetary System," _JMCB_,(Aug.1969), pp. 625-648. (Also, "Comments," pp. 649-680.)

   k. E.A. Birnbaum, "Gold and the International Monetary System: An Orderly Reform," Princeton Univ., _Essays in International Finance_, No.66, April 1969.

      l.   H.G. Johnson, "The Role of Gold," <u>International Currency Review</u>, April 1969.

      m.   Fred Hirsch, "Anatomy of the I.M.F.," Ch. 13 of <u>Money International</u> by F. Hirsch.

      n.   Princeton Series Essays: Nos. 63,70,87,88,89.

  2.   Transition

      a.   *Halm (ed.), entire.

      b.   *J.H. Makin, "Eurocurrencies and the Future of the International Monetary System"(in American Enterprise Inst. Conference, Volume, 1976).

      c.   J.H. Makin, <u>Capital Flows and Exchange Rate Flexibility in the Post-Bretton Woods Era</u> (Princeton: International Finance Section, Feb. 1974).

      d.   J.H. Makin, "Exchange Rate Flexibility and the Demand for International Reserves," <u>Weltwritschaftliches Archiv.</u> Band 110, Heft 2, 1974.

      e.   *E.M. Bernstein, et al., "Reflections on Jamaica," Princeton <u>Essays in International Finance</u>, No. 115, April 1976.

VI. Further Topics on International Monetary Arrangements

  1.   Optimum Currency Areas

      a.   *R.A. Mundell, No. 2, Ch. 12.

      b.   *R.I. McKinnon, No. 4, Ch. 10.

      c.   *H.G. Grubel, "The Theory of Optimum Currency Area," <u>C.J.E.</u> (May 1970).

      d.   T.D. Willett and E. Tower, "Currency Areas and Exchange Rate Flexibility," <u>Weltwirtschaftliches Archiv.</u> (Heft I, 1970), pp. 48-64.

  2.   Experience with Flexible Rates

      a.   *L.B. Yeager, op.cit., Ch.24.

      b.   R.R. Rhomberg, "A Model of the Canadian Economy Under Fixed and Fluctuating Exchange Rates," <u>J.P.E.</u> (Feb,1964), pp. 1-31.

      c.   R.M. Dunn, Jr., <u>Canada's Experience with Fixed and Flexible Exchange Rates in a North American Capital Market,</u> Canadian-American Committee, 1971.

  3.   Princeton Series Essays: Nos. 72,73,78,80,81,83,84.

  4.   More on Exchange Rate Flexibility

      a.   *L.B. Yeager, <u>International Monetary Relations</u>, Chs. 2,10,11,12,13.

b. <u>JMCB</u> (May 1971, Part 2), See Article in Session I, pp. 321-380.

Confidence Problems with the U.S. Dollar as International Money

a. P.B. Kenen, "International Liquidity and the Balance of Payments of a Reserve-Currency Country," <u>Quarterly Journal of Economics</u> (Nov. 1960), pp. 572-586.

b. L.H. Officer and T.D. Willett, "Reserve Asset Preferences and the Confidence Problem in the Crisis Zone," <u>Quarterly Journal of Economics</u> (Nov. 1969), pp. 688-695.

c. J.H. Makin, "Swaps and Roosa Bonds as an Index of the Cost of Co-operation in the 'Crisis Zone'", <u>Quarterly Journal of Economics</u> (May 1971), pp. 349-356.

d. J.H. Makin, "On the Success of the Reserve Currency System in the Crisis Zone," <u>Journal of International Economics</u> (May 1972), pp. 77-86.

6. Special Drawing Rights

a. F. Machlup, "Remaking the International Monetary System: The Rio Agreement and Beyond," (John Hopkins: Baltimore, 1968).

b. J.H. Makin, "The Problem of Coexistence of SDR's and a Reserve Currency," <u>J. of Money, Credit and Banking</u> (Aug. 1972), pp. 509-528.

c. J.H. Makin, "Equilibrium Interest on Special Drawing Rights," <u>Southern Economic Journal</u> (Oct.1974), pp.171-181.

7. Euro-Dollars:

a. *A.K. Swoboda, <u>The Euro-Dollar Market: An Interpretation</u>, Princeton Essays, No. 64.

b. F. Klopstock, <u>The Euro-Dollar Market: Some Unresolved Issues</u>, Princeton Essays, No. 65.

c. *M. Friedman, "The Euro-Dollar Market: Some First Principles," <u>Morgan Guaranty Survey</u> (Oct, 1969), pp.4-14.

d. E. Clodenning, "Euro-Dollars and Credit Creation," <u>International Currency Review</u> (March/April 1971), pp.12-19.

e. F. Machlup, "Euro-Dollar Creation: A Mystery Story," Princeton Reprints in International Finance, No.16, Dec. 1970.

f. *J.H. Makin, "Demand and Supply Functions for Stocks of Euro-Dollar Deposit: An Empirical Study," <u>Review of Economics and Statistics</u> (Nov.1972), pp. 381-391.

g. J.H. Makin, "Identifying a Reserve Base for the Euro-Dollar System," <u>J. of Finance</u> (June 1973).

h. J. Hewson, <u>Liquidity Creation and Distribution in the Eurocurrency Markets</u>, Lexington Books, Lexington, Mass., 1975.

      i.   J.H. Makin, "The 'Multiplier' <u>vs</u> the 'New View' Analysis of Eurocurrencies," in <u>Eurocurrencies and the International Monetary System</u>, C.S. Stern, J.H. Makin and D.E. Logue (eds.).

VII. International Capital Flows

1.   *W.H. Brandson, "Monetary Policy and the New View of International Capital Movements," <u>Brookings Papers on Economic Activity</u>, Vol.2 (1970), pp. 235-270.

2.   *Stern, Chs. 8,9.

3.   *T.D. Willett and F. Forte, "Interest Rate Policy and External Balance," <u>Quarterly Journal of Economics</u> (May,1969) pp. 242-262.

VIII. Growth and the Balance of Payments

1.   *Stern, Ch. 11.

2.   R.A. Mundell, Ch. 9, <u>International Economics</u> (Macmillan: N.Y. 1968).

SUPPLEMENT B TO READING LIST

I.   Contemporary: The Monetary Approach to the Balance of Payments

A. Overview

1.   J.A. Prenkel and H.G. Johnson, "The Monetary Approach to
the Balance of Payments: Essential Concepts and
Historical Origins," in Frenkel and Johnson (1976).

2.   S.P. Magee, "The Empirical Evidence on the Monetary
Approach to the Balance of Payments and Exchange
Rates," American Economic Review (May 1976),
pp. 163-170.

3.   H.G. Johnson V: B,C.

4.   M.V.N. Whitman, "Global Monetarism and the Monetary
Approach to the Balance of Payments," Brookings Papers
3, 1975.

B. Devaluation: Monetary Stock Adjustment (Absorption)

1.   Dornbusch V: H,I.

2.   Alexander V: K.

3.   Mussa V: J.

4.   Kemp V: *K.

C. Devaluation: Flow, Trade-Balance Adjustment ("Elasticity")

1.   Tsiang IV: H,I. (Also in AEA "Readings,"eds. Caves and
Johnson.)

2.   Joan Robinson, "The Foreign Exchanges," In AEA "Readings"
eds. Ellis and Metzler.

II. General Equilibrium Models for Investigation of Monetary
Disturbances in Open Economics

A. Early papers on the role of monetary policy under fixed/
floating exchange rates

1.   M. Fleming, "Domestic Financial Policies under Fixed and
Floating Exchange Rates," I.M.F. Staff Papers (1962),
pp. 362-79.

2.   R.A. Mundell, "Flexible Exchange Rates and Employment
Policy," Canadian Journal of Economics and Political
Science (Nov. 1961), pp. 509-17.

Note: * These papers will be distributed

B. Contemporary Overview

1. A. Lindbeck, "Approaches to Exchange Rate Analysis:
An Introduction," <u>Scandinavian Journal of Economics</u>,
1976, pp. 133-145.

C. Re-examination of the efficacy of monetary policy under
fixed/floating exchange rates

1. Niehans, IV: H.7.

2. Dornbusch, IV: H.6.

3. Connolly and Taylor, IV: H.8.

D. The need to consider supply side effects of devaluation

1. Makin, "On the Relative Efficacy of Monetary Policy
Under Flexible Exchange Rates: Some Supply Considerations."

2. Makin, "Anticipated Inflation and Interest Rates in an
Open Economy (to be read as background for Ch.1).

3. Dornbusch and Krugman, "Flexible Exchange Rates in the
Short Run," <u>Brookings Papers on Economic Activity</u> 3,
1976, pp. 537-84.

III. Insulation and Interdependence under Fixed and Floating Exchange
Rates

A. Classics

1. S. Laursen and L.A. Metzler, "Flexible Exchange Rates
and the Theory of Employment," <u>The Review of Economics
and Statistics</u> (November 1950), pp. 281-99.

2. A.C. Harberger, "Currency Depreciation, Income and the
Balance of Trade," <u>Journal of Political Economy</u>
(Feb.1950), pp. 47-60.

3. F. Machlup, "Relative Prices and Aggregate Spending in
the Analysis of Devaluation," <u>American Economic Review</u>
(June 1955), pp. 255-78.

B. Keynesian

1. Mundell, IV: G.1.

2. Cooper, IV: G.2.

C. Keynesian/Monetary

1. Makin, "A General Model for Analysis of Open Economics".

2. Kemp IV: *K (already assigned in Section I, B.)

B. A. 287 – International Financial Management
Mr. Kohlhagen

Prerequisite: B. A. 130G and B. A. 285.

Required Texts:

David K. Eiteman and Arthur I. Stonehill, Multinational Business Finance, Addison-Wesley, 1979. [ES]

Donald R. Lessard, International Financial Management: Theory and Application. Warren, Gorham, and Lamont, 1979. [Lessard]

Recommend Reading:

Paul E. Erdman, The Billion Dollar Sure Thing. Pocket Books, 1973.

Paul E. Erdman, The Crash of '79.

(* denotes a required reading)
((P) denotes on Personal Copy Reserve)

I. The Scope of International Financial Management

    * ES, Chapter 1

II. Foreign Exchange Rate Determination and Forecasting

    A. The Foreign Exchange Markets

*	ES, Chapter 2.	
	Coninx, Raymond.	Foreign Exchange Today. Woodhead-Faulkner, 1978. Chapters 7-8.
(P)	Kubarych, Roger M.	Foreign Exchange Markets in the U.S. Federal Reserve Bank of New York, 1978.
	Group of Thirty.	Foreign Exchange Markets Under Floating Rates. 1980.
*(P)	Kohlhagen, Steven W.	"The Experience With Floating: The 1973-1979 Dollar."
(P)	Frenkel, Jacob A.	"Flexible Exchange Rates, Prices and the Role of 'News': Lessons from the 1970's."
	Hooper, Peter, and Steven W. Kohlhagen.	"The Effects of Exchange Rate Uncertainty on the Volume and Prices of International Trade." Journal of International Economics, November 1978.
	Kohlhagen, Steven W.	"The Identification of Destabilizing Foreign Exchange Speculation." Journal of International Economics, August 1979.
	Ensor, Richard.	"The World's Best Foreign Exchange Dealer." Euromoney, September 1980.
	Borsuk, Mark.	"The New Law Leaves the Yen a Long Way from Internationalization." Euromoney, July 1979.
	Nakamae, Tadashi.	"The Coming World Role of the Yen." Euromoney, September 1980, pp. 18-19.
	Babbel, David.	"The Rise and Decline of Foreign Currency Options." Euromoney, September 1980.
	Levi, Maurice D.	"Taxation and 'Abnormal' International Capital Flows." In Lessard, pp. 309 ff.

    B. The Determination of the Exchange Rate

*	Dornbusch, Rudiger.	"Exchange Rate Economics: Where Do We Stand?" Brookings Papers on Economic Activity, 1: 1980, George L. Perry, ed., pp. 143-185.

Ian H. Giddy.   "An Integrated Theory of Exchange Rate Equilibrium." In Lessard, pp. 167-176.

*   Dornbusch, Rudiger.   "Exchange Rate Dynamics." <u>Journal of Political Economy</u>, December 1976, 1161-1176.

*   Frenkel, Jacob A.   "A Monetary Approach to the Exchange Rate: Doctrinal Aspects and Empirical Evidence." In Lessard, pp. 177-202.

Aliber, Robert Z.   "The Interest Rate Parity Theorem: A Reinterpretation." <u>Journal of Political Economy</u>, December 1973, 1451-1459.

Kohlhagen, Steven W.   <u>The Behavior of Foreign Exchange Markets--A Critical Survey of the Empirical Literature</u>. New York University Monograph Series in Finance and Economics, 1978.

*   McKinnon, Ronald I.   <u>Money in International Exchange: The Convertible Currency System</u>. Oxford University Press, 1979. Whole book; *Chapter 6.

*   Bilson, John.   "The Monetary Approach to the Exchange Rate: Some Empirical Evidence." <u>IMF Staff Papers</u>, 1978.

*   Frankel, J. A.   "On the Mark: A Theory of Floating Exchange Rates Based on Real Interest Differentials." <u>American Economic Review</u>, September 1979, 610-622.

Grubel, Herbert.   <u>Forward Exchange, Speculation and the International Flow of Capital</u>. Stanford University Press, 1966, pp. 3-55.

*   Levich, Richard.   Chapter 8 in Jacob A. Frenkel and Harry G. Johnson, <u>The Economics of Exchange Rates</u>. Addison-Wesley, 1978.

*   Dooley, Michael P., and Peter Isard.   "Capital Controls, Political Risk, and Deviations from Interest-Rate Parity." <u>Journal of Political Economy</u>, April 1980, pp. 370-384.

*   Stockman, Alan C.   "A Theory of Exchange Rate Determination." <u>Journal of Political Economy</u>, August 1980, pp. 673-698.

Isard, Peter.   "How Far Can We Push the Law of One Price?" <u>American Economic Review</u>, December 1977.

_____.   <u>Exchange Rate Determination: A Survey of Popular Views and Recent Models</u>. Princeton Studies in International Finance No. 42. International Finance Section, Princeton University, 1978.

Dornbusch, Rudiger.   Chapter 2 in Jacob A. Frenkel and Harry G. Johnson, The Economics of Exchange Rates. Addison-Wesley, 1978.

Hodrick, Robert J.   Chapter 6 in Jacob A. Frenkel and Harry G. Johnson, The Economics of Exchange Rates. Addison-Wesley, 1978.

C. Exchange Rate Forecasting

*(P) Levich, Richard.   "Analyzing the Accuracy of Foreign Exchange Advisory Services: Theory and Evidence."

* Goodman, Stephen.   "Foreign Exchange Rate Forecasting Techniques: Implications for Business and Policy." Journal of Finance, May 1979, 415.

Everett, Robert M., George Abraham, and Aryeh Blumberg.   "Appraising Currency Strengths and Weaknesses: An Operational Model for Calculating Parity Exchange Rates." Journal of International Business Studies, Fall, 1980, pp. 80-91.

Bilson, John.   "Leading Indicators of Currency Revaluation." Columbia Journal of World Business, Winter, 1979, pp. 62-76.

* Euromoney   "Judgment Day for the Forecasters." September 1980.

* Goodman, Stephen H.   "Who's Better Than the Toss of a Coin?" Euromoney, September 1980.

Nakamae, T.   "Is the Yen Easily Predictable?" Euromoney, March 1980.

D. Exchange Rate Efficiency

* Frenkel, Jacob A., and Michael L. Mussa   "The Efficiency of Foreign Exchange Markets and Measures of Turbulence." American Economic Review, May 1980, pp. 374-381.

Frenkel, Jacob A.   "Efficiency and Volatility of Exchange Rates and Prices in the 1970s." Columbia Journal of World Business, Winter, 1979, pp. 15-27.

King, David.   "Exchange Market Efficiency and the Risk-Taker of Last Resort." Columbia Journal of World Business, Winter, 1979, pp. 28-35.

*   Levich, Richard.   "Are Forward Exchange Rates Unbiased Predictors of Future Spot Rates?" <u>Columbia Journal of World Business</u>, Winter, 1979, pp. 49-61.

*   Levich, Richard M.   "The Efficiency of Markets for Foreign Exchange: A Review and Extension." In Lessard, pp. 243 ff.

     Frenkel, Jacob A., and Richard M. Levich.   "Transactions Costs and Interest Arbitrage: Tranquil Versus Turbulent Periods." In Lessard, pp. 277 ff.

III. Defining Exposure to Exchange Risk

   *   Ankrom, Robert K.   "Top-Level Approach to Foreign Exchange Rate Problem." In Lessard, pp. 381 ff.

   *   Shank, John K.   "FASB Statement 8 Resolved Foreign Currency Accounting—Or Did It?" In Lessard, pp. 435 ff.

   *   Logue, Dennis E. and Oldfield, George S.   "Managing Foreign Assets When Foreign Exchange Markets are Efficient." In Lessard, pp. 367 ff.

   *   ES, Chapter 3.

        Dufey, Gunter.   "Corporate Finance and Exchange Rate Variations." In Lessard, pp. 391-398.

        Heckerman, Donald.   "The Exchange Risk of Foreign Operations." In Lessard, pp. 399-408.

        Frederickson, E. Bruce   "On the Measurement of Foreign Income." In Lessard, pp. 409-424.

   *   Aliber, Robert Z. and Stickney, Clyde P.   "Accounting Measures for Foreign Exchange Exposure: The Long and Short of It." In Lessard, pp. 425-434.

        Carter, E. and Rodriguez, R.   "What 40 U.S. Multinationals Think." Euromoney, March, 1978.

  (P)   Financial Accounting Standards Board.   Accounting for Foreign Currency Translation. 1979.

        _____ _____.   Statement of Financial Accounting Standards. #8, October, 1975.

  (P)   Wihlborg, Clas A.   "Currency Exposure: Taxonomy and Theory."

  (P)   Folks, William and Evans.   "The Impact of FASB #8 on Corporate Exchange Risk Management: The Rational Firm's Response to Foreign Exchange Risk," 1979.

*(P)   Dukes, Roland E.   "Forecasting Exchange Gains (Losses) and Security Market Responses to FASB Statement #8."

        Choi, Fred, Lowe, H. and Worthley, R.   "Accountors, Accountants and Standard #8." Journal of International Business Studies, Fall, 1978.

*(P)   Hodder, James E.   "Exposure to Exchange Rate Movements."

IV. Managing Exchange Exposure

      *   ES, Chapter 4.

      *   Kohlhagen, Steven.   "Reducing Foreign Exchange Risks." _Columbia Journal of W. Business_, Spring, 1978.

              ————————.   "A Model of Optimal Foreign Exchange Hedging without Exchange Rate Projections." _Journal of International Business Studies_, Fall, 1978.

          Levi, Maurice D.   "Underutilization of Forward Markets as Rational Behavior?" _Journal of Finance_, September, 1979. 1013.

          Rosenwald, Roger W.   "How to Use the Various Definitions of Exposure." _Euromoney_, December, 1976.

          Thunnel, Lars.   "The American Express Formula." _Euromoney_, March, 1980.

      *   Lessard, Donald R.   "Introduction to Financial Management of International Operations." In Lessard, pp. 349-366.

      *   Giddy, Ian H.   "Why It Doesn't Pay to Make a Habit of Forward Hedging." In Lessard, pp. 375 ff.

          Shapiro, Alan C. and Rutenberg, David P.   "Managing Exchange Risks in a Floating World." In Lessard, pp. 443 ff.

      *   Makin, John H.   "Portfolio Theory and the Problem of Foreign Exchange Risk." In Lessard, pp. 455 ff.

    *(P) Levi, Maurice D.   "Optimal Hedging Behavior and the Exporting Firm."

V. Foreign Investment

      *   ES, Chapter 7.

          Kindleberger, Charles P.   "The Theory of Direct Investment." In Lessard, pp. 19-30.

          Ragazzi, Giorgio.   "Theories of the Determinants of Direct Foreign Investment." In Lessard, pp. 31-56.

          Magee, Stephen P.   "Information and the Multinational Corporation: An Appropriability Theory of Direct Foreign Investment." In Lessard, pp. 57-82.

VI.   Capital Budgeting

    *   ES, Chapter 8.

Shapiro, Alan C.	"Capital Budgeting for the Multinational Cor- poration." In Lessard, pp. 567 ff.
Lessard, Donald R.	"Evaluating Foreign Projects: An Adjusted Present Value Approach." In Lessard, pp. 577 ff.

VII. International Capital Markets

    *   ES, Chapter 9.

Friedman, Milton.	"The Eurodollar Market: Some First Principles." Federal Reserve Bank of St. Louis, <u>Review</u>. June, 1969.
Mills, Rodney H. and Short, Eugenie.	<u>U.S. Banks and the North American European Cur- rency Market</u>. International Finance Dis- cussion Papers, #134.
Robbins, Stobaugh, et alii.	<u>How to Use International Capital Markets: A Guide to Europe and the Middle East</u>. Fin. Exec. Research Foundation, 1976.
U.S. Government Printing Office.	<u>The Eurocurrency Market Control Act of 1979</u>. Committee on Banking, Finance and Urban Affairs. Serial No. 96-23.
* <u>Columbia Journal of World Business</u>.	"The Euromarket." Fall, 1979.
<u>Euromoney</u>.	"How Bankers in Tokyo are Living through the Freeze." February, 1980.
* <u>Euromoney</u>.	"The Coming Revolution in Investment Banking." March, 1980.
<u>FRBNY Quarterly Review</u>.	"The Debate over Regulating the Eurocurrency Markets." Winter, 1979.
Mills, Rodney H.	"U.S. Banks are Losing Their Share of the Market." <u>Euromoney</u>. February, 1980.
Prindl, Andreas R.	"Japan is Liberalizing the Wrong Things." <u>Euromoney</u>. March, 1980.
(P) Heller, H. R.	"Money and Credit in the Euromarkets: A Demand Approach." August, 1979.
* Rodriguez, Rita M. and Carter, E. Eugene.	<u>International Financial Management</u>. Prentice-Hall 2nd ed., 1979. Chapter 15.

VIII.   Managing Political Risk

    *   ES, Chapters 5, 6.

Choi, Fred and Mueller, G.	An Introduction to Multinational Accounting. Prentice-Hall, 1978. Chapter 7.
Ball, Robert.	"The Unseemly Squabble over Iran's Assets." Fortune, January 28, 1980.
Eiteman, David and Stonehill, Arthur.	"Why Did Chase Move so Fast?" Euromoney, January, 1980.

IX.   Capital Market Integration, International Portfolio Diversification, Cost of Capital

    *   ES, Chapter 10.

Robbins, Sidney M. and Stobaugh, Robert B.	"Financing Foreign Affiliates." In Lessard, pp. 593 ff.
Naumann-Etienne, Rudiger.	"A Framework for Financial Decisions in Multinational Corporations—A Summary of Recent Research." In Lessard, pp. 603 ff.
* Shapiro, Alan C.	"Financial Structure and Cost of Capital in the Multinational Corporation." Journal of Financial and Quantitative Analysis, June 1978. pp. 211-226.
Mehra, Rajnish.	"On the Financing and Investment Decisions of Multinational Firms in the Presence of Exchange Risk." Journal of Financial and Quantitative Analysis, June, 1978, 227-244.
Folks, William.	"Optimal Foreign Borrowing Strategies with Operations in Forward Exchange Markets." Journal of Financial and Quantitative Analysis, June, 197
Black, Fischer.	"The Ins and Outs of Foreign Investment." In Lessard, pp. 5 ff.
* Solnik, Bruno.	"Why Not Diversify Internationally Rather than Domestically?" In Lessard, pp. 13 ff.
Stehle, Richard.	"An Empirical Test of the Alternative Hypotheses of National and International Pricing of Risky Assets." In Lessard, pp. 145 ff.
* Cooper, Richard N.	"Towards an International Capital Market?" In Lessard, pp. 83 ff.

*   Lessard, Donald R.   "World, Country, and Industry Relationships in Equity Returns: Implications for Risk Reduction through International Diversification." In Lessard, pp. 101 ff.

*   Black, Fischer.   "International Capital Market Equilibrium with Investment Barriers." In Lessard, pp. 119 ff.

Cohn, Richard A. and Pringle, John J.   "Imperfections in International Financial Markets: Implications for Risk Premia and the Cost of Capital to Firms." In Lessard, pp. 109 ff.

Stapleton, R. C. and Subrahmanyam, M. G.   "Market Imperfections, Capital Market Equilibrium, and Corporation Finance." In Lessard, pp. 135 ff.

Heckerman, Donald.   "On the Effects of Exchange Risk." In Lessard, pp. 321 ff.

Grauer, Frederick L. A., Litzenberger, Robert H., and Stehle, Richard E.   "Sharing Rules and Equilibrium in an International Capital Market under Uncertainty: An Abrigement." In Lessard, pp. 331 ff.

*(P) Lessard, Donald R.   "International Diversification." In The Investment Manager's Handbook, 1980.

*(P) Kohlhagen, Steven W.   "Overlapping National Investment Portfolios: Evidence and Implications of International Integration of Secondary Assets for Financial Markets."

*   Euromoney.   "Why Americans Should Have Diversified." March, 1980.

*   Frankel, J. A.   "The Diversifiability of Exchange Risk." Journal of International Economics, August, 1979.

Grubel, H. G. and Fadner, K.   "The Interdependence of International Equity Markets." Journal of Finance, March, 1971.

Lessard, Donald R.   "International Portfolio Diversification: A Multivariate Analysis for a Group of Latin American Countries." Journal of Finance, June, 1973, 619-633.

Levy, Haim, and Sarnat, M.   "International Diversification of Investment Portfolios." American Economic Review, September 1970, 668-675.

Guy, James R. F.   "An Examination of the Effects of International Diversification from the British Viewpoint on Both Hypothetical and Real Portfolios." Journal of Finance, December 1978, 1425-1438.

————————.   "The Performance of the British Investment Trust Industry." Journal of Finance, May 1978, 443-456.

Remmers, H. Lee.   "A Note on Foreign Borrowing Costs," Journal of International Business Studies, Fall, 1980, pp. 123-134.

X. Working Capital Management

    * ES, Chapters 11-13.

XI. Export-Import Financing

    * ES, Chapter 14.

      U.S. Customs Service, <u>Exporting to the United States</u>.
      U.S. Treasury.

XII. Accounting

    * ES, Chapter 15.

      Choi, Fred and <u>An Introduction to Multinational Accounting</u>.
      Mueller, G.   Prentice-Hall, 1978.

      Price Waterhouse. "A Survey in 46 Countries." <u>Accounting Principles
                   and Reporting Practices</u>, 1975.

XIII. Taxation

    * ES, Chapter 16.

    * Shapiro, Alan C. "Evaluating Financing Costs for Multinational
                   Subsidiaries." In Lessard, pp. 475 ff.

      Barrett, M. Edgar. "Case of the Tangled Transfer Price." In Lessard,
                   pp. 485 ff.

      Lall, Sanjaya. "Transfer-Pricing by Multinational Manufacturing
                   Firms." In Lessard, pp. 495 ff.

    * Horst, Thomas. "American Taxation of Multinational Firms." In
                   Lessard, pp. 517 ff.

      Rutenberg, David P. "Maneuvering Liquid Assets in a Multi-National
                   Company: Formulation and Determining
                   Solution Procedures." In Lessard, pp.
                   531 ff.

      Robbins, Sidney M. and "The Bent Measuring Stick for Foreign Subsidiaries."
      Stobaugh, Robert B.   In Lessard, pp. 547 ff.

B40.3383   Richard Levich
International Financial Markets   Spring 1981

This course examines both positive and normative aspects of international financial markets. In Section I, we develop models of the international monetary system and several of its important components. Here the emphasis is on positive economics -- What are the fundamental determinants of the balance of payments, of spot and forward exchange rates, and of domestic, foreign and Euro-currency interest rates? What are the characteristics of equilibrium among these variables and how does the system respond to exogenous disturbances? This section also explores several other important but more specialized topics including transaction costs in international markets, the efficient market hypothesis in international markets, the nature of foreign exchange risk, government intervention and capital controls. We proceed to examine the determinants of long term international capital flows which leads to a discussion of the relation between national equity markets and the nature of international portfolio diversification. Institutional characteristics of the markets are also presented.

In Section II we build on the theoretical base of Section I and focus our attention more on policy issues. The relationship between the organization of the international monetary system and macroeconomic aggregates is discussed. Here the issues include (1) the choice of exchange rate systems, (2) the gains from common currency areas and (3) the distributional effects of seignorage.

Many of the topics in this course are relevant for international financial management policy by an individual investor or firm. Since these topics are the subject of another course (B40.3385), they will be discussed only in passing. Students are encouraged to ask questions whenever theory of applications are unclear.

Materials Available for Purchase   (Abbreviation)

Required Purchase

   R. Aliber, The International Money Game, Third Edition, Basic Books, 1979.

   G. Dufey and I. Giddy, The International Money Market, Prentice Hall, 1978.

   D. Lessard (ed.), International Financial Management, Warren, Gorham and
                     Lamont, 1979. (IFM)

   Packet of Readings

Optional Purchase

   J. Frenkel and H. Johnson, The Economics of Exchange Rates, Addison-Wesley

   E. Sohmen, Flexible Exchange Rates, University of Chicago Press, 1969.

   R. McKinnon, The Eurocurrency Market, Princeton Essays in International
         Finance, No. 125, December 1977.

P. Isard, Exchange-Rate Determination: A Survey of Popular Views and
Recent Models, Princeton Studies in International Finance, No. 42,
May 1978.

S. Kohlhagen, The Behavior of Foreign Exchange Markets: A Critical Survey
of the Empirical Literature, New York University, Salomon Brothers
Center Monograph Series in Finance and Economics, No. 1978-3, 1978.

Course Outline and Reading List

Try to read The International-Money Game by the second week of the semester.
It covers many of the issues we will examine in this course. Readings marked by
(*) are required. This set of readings should prepare you for the course examinati
Readings marked by (P) are in the packet of readings which can be purchased at the
Bookstore. Readings marked by (R) should be available in the reserve library.
A second extended reading list containing articles of historical interest or artic
presenting current research in more specialized areas will be distributed upon req

I. International Financial Markets--Theoretical Issues and Evidence

   A. Overview of the International Financial System: Current Problems and Issu

      * Robert Z. Aliber, The International Money Game

      * Economic Report of the President, 1980, Chapter 4, pp. 156-183. (R)

      * Scott Pardee, "How Well Are the Exchange Markets Functioning," FRB of
          N.Y. Quarterly Review 4, No. 1 (Spring 1979): 49-52. (P)

      * Holmes and Pardee, "Treasury and Federal Reserve Foreign Exchange
          Operations," FRB of N.Y. Quarterly Review 4, No. 1 (Spring 1979):
          67-87. (P)

        International Monetary Fund, Annual Report, 1980. (R)

   B. Balance of Payments Accounting and Concepts

      * Robert M. Stern, The Balance of Payments, Chapter 1. (P)

      * Donald Kemp, "Balance of Payments Concepts--What Do They Really Mean?
          Monthly Review, FRB of St. Louis, April 1975. (P)

        Rita Maldonado, "Review of the Report," Journal of Economic Literatu
          15, No. 2 (June 1977): 555-58.

        Robert M. Stern, et al., The Presentation of the U.S. Balance of
          Payments: A Symposium, Princeton Essays in International Finance
          No. 123, August 1977. (R)

C. The Building Blocks

1. Monetary Theory of the Balance of Payments

   * Donald Kemp, "A Monetary View of the Balance of Payments," _Monthly Review_, FRB of St. Louis, July 1975. (P)

   Jacob A. Frenkel and Harry G. Johnson, "The Monetary Approach to the Balance of Payments: Essential Concepts and Historical Origins." In Frenkel and Johnson, eds., _The Monetary Approach to the Balance of Payments_, 1976. (R)

   Kreinin and Officer, _The Monetary Approach to the Balance of Payments: A Survey_, Princeton Studies in International Finance, No. 43, November 1978. (R)

2. Purchasing Power Parity

   * Ronald I. McKinnon, _Money in International Exchange_, Chapter 6, pp. 117-41. (P)

   Bela Balassa, "The Purchasing Power Parity Doctrine: A Reappraisal," _Journal of Political Economy_ 72, No. 6 (December 1964): 584-96.

   Robert Z. Lawrence, "Within and Between Country Variances in Inflation Rates: Are They Similar?" _Journal of Monetary Economics_ 5, No. 1 (January 1979): 145-52.

   "Purchasing Power Parity: A Symposium, "_Journal of International Economics_ 8, No. 2 (May 1978).

3. Fisher Closed and Fisher Open

   * Aliber and Stickney, "Accounting Measures of Foreign Exchange Exposure: The Long and Short of It," in _IFM_, Chapter 28.

   Eugene Fama, "Short-Term Interest Rates as Predictors of Inflation," _American Economic Review_, (June 1975): 269-82.

   Michael Porter, "A Theoretical and Empirical Framework for Analyzing the Term Structure of Exchange Rate Expectations," _IMF Staff Papers_, (November 1971): 613-45.

4. Interest Rate Parity Theory

   See Articles under Section G.

D. Theories of the Fundamental Determinants of Exchange Rates

* Ian Giddy, "An Integrated Theory of Exchange Rate Equilibrium," in
    IFM, Chapter 13.

* Bruno Solnik, "International Parity Conditions and Exchange Risk:
    A Review," Journal of Banking and Finance 2, No. 3 (October 1978):
    281-294. (P)

* Rudiger Dornbusch, "Monetary Policy Under Exchange-Rate Flexibility,"
    in IFM Chapter 15.

  Peter Isard, Exchange Rate Determination: A Survey of Popular Views
    and Recent Models. Princeton Studies in International Finance,
    No. 42, May 1978. (R)

  Susan Schadler, "Sources of Exchange Rate Variability: Theory and
    Empirical Evidence," IMF Staff Papers, July 1977.

1. The Monetary Approach

* Jacob Frenkel, "A Monetary Approach to the Exchange Rate: Doctrinal
    Aspects and Empirical Evidence," in IFM, Chapter 14.

  Rudiger Dornbusch, "The Theory of Flexible Exchange Rate Regimes and
    Macroeconomic Policy." Chapter 2 in The Economics of Exchange
    Rates. (R)

2. Rational Expectations and Exchange Rate Dynamics

  John Bilson, "Rational Expectations and the Exchange Rate." Chapter 5
    in The Economics of Exchange Rates. (R)

* Rudiger Dornbusch, "Expectations and Exchange Rate Dynamics," Journal
    of Political Economy, December 1976. (P)

* Richard Levich, "An Examination of Overshooting Behavior in the Foreign
    Exchange Market," Group of 30 manuscript, 1980. (P)

  Bradford Cornell, "Relative Price Changes and Deviations from Purchasing
    Power Parity," Journal of Banking and Finance 3, No. 3
    (September 1979): 263-280.

  Rudiger Dornbusch, "Exchange Rate Economics: Where Do We Stand?"
    Brookings Papers on Economic Activity, 1980, No. 1 (P).

3. Portfolio Balance Models

  William Branson, "Exchange Rate Dynamics and Monetary Policy." Chapter 8
    in Assar Lindbeck (ed.), Inflation and Employment in Open Economies,
    1979.

Pentti Kouri, "The Exchange Rate and the Balance of Payments in the Short Run and in the Long Run." <u>Scandinavian Journal of Economics</u> 78, No. 2 (May 1976): 280-304.

E. The Foreign Exchange Market

1. History, Institutional Organization, Basic Terminology

   * Roger Kubarych, <u>Foreign Exchange Markets in the United States</u>. FRBNY 1978. (Distributed in class).

2. Participants, Market-making, Transaction Costs

   Norman Fieleke, "Exchange Rate Flexibility and the Efficiency of the Foreign Exchange Markets," <u>Journal of Financial and Quantitative Analysis</u> 10, No. 3-5 (September 1975): 409-26.

   Frank McCormick, "Covered Interest Arbitrage: Unexploited Profits?: Comment," <u>Journal of Political Economy</u> 87, No. 2 (April 1979): 411-17.

   William Allen, "A Note on Uncertainty, Transaction Costs and Interest Parity," <u>Journal of Monetary Economics</u>, No. 3 (1977): 367-73.

3. International Banks and Foreign Exchange Trading

   Andrew Brimmer, "The Federal Reserve and the Failure of Franklin National Bank," in Backman (ed.), <u>Business and the American Economy</u>, 1776-2001.

   Dreyer, Haberler and Willett (eds.), <u>Exchange Rate Flexibility</u>, 1978. Especially Part II.

4. Chicago's International Money Market

F. Foreign Exchange Market Efficiency on Theory and Evidence

   * Richard Levich, "The Efficiency of Markets for Foreign Exchange: A Review and Extension," in <u>IFM</u>, Chapter 16.

   Steven Kohlhagen, <u>The Behavior of Foreign Exchange Markets--A Critical Survey of the Empirical Literature</u>, Salomon Brothers Center Monograph Series, New York University, No. 1978-3, 1978.

G. Covered Interest Arbitrage and Interest Parity Theory

      * Robert Aliber, "The Interest Rate Parity Theorem: A Reinterpretation," Journal of Political Economy (Nov./De. 1973): 1451-59. (P)

      Frenkel and Levich, "Covered Interest Arbitrage: Unexploited Profits?" Journal of Political Economy (April 1975): 325-38.

      * Maurice Levi, "Taxation and Abnormal International Capital Flows," in IFM, Chapter 19.

      * Frenkel and Levich, "Transaction Costs and Interest Arbitrage: Tranquil versus Turbulent Periods," in IFM, Chapter 17.

      Alan Deardorff, "One-Way Arbitrage and Its Implications for the Foreign Exchange Markets," Journal of Political Economy (April 1979): 351-64.

H. Eurocurrencies -- The External Currency Markets

    1. First Principles, Institutions, Growth of the Market

      * Dufey and Giddy, The International Money Market, Chapters 1, 5.

      * Andrew Crockett, "The Euro-Currency Market: An Attempt to Clarify Some Basic Issues," International Monetary Fund Staff Papers, July 1976. (P)

      Ronald McKinnon, The Eurocurrency Market. Princeton Essays in International Finance, No. 125, December 1977. (R)

    2. Determination of Offshore Rates, Market Size and Location and Transaction Co

      * Dufey and Giddy, Chapters 2, 3.

    3. Offshore Markets, International Markets and U.S. Monetary Policy

      * Dufey and Giddy, Chapters 4, 6

I. The Forward Rate, Speculation and Foreign Exchange Risk

    1. Determination of the Forward Rate

      Egon Sohmen, Flexible Exchange Rates, Chapter 4. (R)

      S.C. Tsiang, "The Theory of Forward Exchange and Effects of Government Intervention on the Forward Exchange Market," International Monetary Fund Staff Papers, (April 1959): 75-106.

    2. The Concept of Exchange Risk

      Jeffrey Frankel, "The Diversifiability of Exchange Risk," Journal of International Economics (August 1979): 379-93.

3. The Forward Rate and Exchange Rate Forecasting

   * Bradford Cornell, "Spot Rates, Forward Rates and Market Efficiency," in IFM, Chapter 18.

   * Richard Levich, "Analyzing the Accuracy of Foreign Exchange Advisory Services: Theory and Evidence," in Levich and Wihlborg (eds.), Exchange Risk and Exposure, 1980. (P)

   * Richard Levich, "Are Forward Rates Unbiased Predictors of Future Spot Rates," Columbia Journal of World Business, (Winter 1979. (P)

   * John Bilson, "Leading Indicators of Currency Devaluation," Columbia Journal of World Business, Winter 1979. (P)

4. Stabilizing and Destabilizing Speculation

   * Steven Kohlhagen, "The Identification of Destabilizing Foreign Exchange Speculation," Journal of International Economics, 9, No. 4 (August 1978) 321-40. (P)

   Egon Sohmen, Flexible Exchange Rates, Chapter 3 (R)

5. Macroeconomic Effects of Exchange Risk

   * Donald Heckerman, "On the Effects of Exchange Risk," in IFM, Chapter 20.

   Hooper and Kohlhagen, "The Effect of Exchange Rate Uncertainty on the Prices and Volume of International Trade," Journal of International Economics 8, No. 4 (November 1978) 483-522.

   Mordechai Kreinin, "The Effect of Exchange Rate Changes on the Prices and Volume of Foreign Trade," International Monetary Fund Staff Papers 24, No. 2 (July 1977): 297-329.

J. Government Intervention and Capital Controls

   1. The Snake and Managed Floating

      * A. James Meigs, "The Role of Information Disclosure in International Monetary Policy" in Richard D. Erb (ed.), Federal Reserve Policies and Public Disclosure, Washington, D.C.: American Enterprises Institute, 1978. (P)

      Helmut Mayer, The Anatomy of Official Exchange-Rate Intervention Systems, Princeton Essays in International Finance, No. 104, May 1974. (R)

      * Stanley Black, "Central Bank Intervention and the Stability of Exchange Rates," in Levich and Wihlborg (eds), Exchange Risk and Exposure, 1980. (P)

IMF _Survey_, Supplement: The European Monetary System, March 19, 1979.

Wilson Schmidt, "Foreign Exchange Intervention by the Federal Reserve Bank of New York: Some Questions." In Dreyer, Haberler and Willett (eds.), _Exchange Rate Flexibility_. Washington, D.C.: American Enterprise Institute, 1978. (R)

Wall Street Journal, "How to Defend the Dollar." November 4, 1977, p. 12

Anatol Balbach, "The Mechanics of Intervention in Exchange Markets," _Monthly Review_, Federal Reserve Bank of St. Louis, 60, No. 2 (February 1978): 2-7.

Roger Kubarych, "Monetary Effects of Federal Reserve Swaps," _Quarterly Review_, Federal Reserve Bank of New York, 2, No. 4 (Winter 1977-78): 19-21.

2. Surveillance

   Thomas Willett, "Alternative Approaches to International Surveillance of Exchange-Rate Policies," in _Managed Exchange Rate Flexibility_, FRB of Bo

   Artus and Crockett, _Floating Exchange Rates and the Need for Surveillance_ Princeton Essays in International Finance, No. 127, May 1978. (R)

3. Counter Speculation

4. Capital Controls - Description, Theory and Empirical Tests

   IMF, _Annual Report of Exchange Restrictions_, 1979, pp. 3-30.

   IMF, _Survey_, August 14, 1978.

   E. Clendenning, _The Euro-Dollar Market_, Appendices A, E, F.

   A. Cairncross, _Control of Long-Term International Capital Movements_, The Brookings Institution, 1973.

   * Dooley and Isard, "Capital Controls, Political Risk, and Deviations from Interest Rate Parity," _Journal of Political Economy_ (April 1980): 370-

5. Capital Controls - Welfare Effects

   Norman Fieleke, _The Welfare Effects of Controls over Capital Exports from the United States_, Princeton Essay in International Finance, No. 82, January 1971.

K. Long-Term Capital Flows

1. Direct Foreign Investment Flows

   * Giorgio Ragazzi, "Theories of the Determinants of Direct Foreign Investment," in IFM, Chapter 4.

2. Portfolio Theory and International Markets

   * Herbert Grubel, "Internationally Diversified Portfolios," AER, December 1968, pp. 1299-1314. (P)

   Levy and Sarnat, "International Diversification of Investment Portfolios," American Economic Review, September 1970, pp. 668-675.

   * Bruno Solnik, "Why Not Diversify Internationally Rather Than Domestically?" in IFM, Chapter 2.

3. Capital Market Theory and International Asset Pricing

   Bruno Solnik, "An Equilibrium Model of the International Capital Market," Journal of Economic Theory, August 1974, pp. 500-524.

   * Donald Lessard, "World, Country and Industry Relationships in Equity Returns," in IFM, Chapter 7.

   Grauer, Litzenberger and Stehle, "Sharing Rules ..." in IFM, Chapter 21.

   Richard Stehle, in IFM, Chapter 11.

4. Efficiency of Foreign Equity Markets

   Bruno Solnik, "Note on the Validity of the Random Walk for European Stock Prices," Journal of Finance, December 1973, pp. 1151-1159.

   John McDonald, "French Mutual Fund Performance: Evaluation of Internationally Diversified Portfolios," Journal of Finance, December 1973, pp. 1161-1180.

   Ian Giddy, Devaluations, Revaluations, and Stock Market Prices, Ph.D. thesis, University of Michigan, 1974.

L. International Financial Market Integration

   * Peter Kenen, Capital Mobility and Financial Integration: A Survey, Princeton Studies in International Finance, No. 39, December 1976. (R)

   Richard Cooper, "Towards an International Capital Market?" in IFM, Chapter 6.

Tamir Agmon, "The Relationship Among Equity Markets: A Study of Share Price Co-Movements in the U.S., U.K., Germany and Japan," Journal of Finance, September 1972, pp. 839-855.

Logue, Salant and Sweeney, "International Integration of Financial Markets: Survey Synthesis and Results," in Eurocurrencies and the International Monetary System, 1976, pp. 91-137.

II. Macroeconomic Policy Issues in International Finance

A. Exchange Rate Systems

* Artus and Young, "Fixed and Flexible Rates: A Renewal of the Debate," IMF Staff Papers (December 1979): 654-98. (P)

* H.G. Johnson, "The Case for Flexible Exchange Rates, 1969," Monthly Review, FRB of St. Louis, June 1969, pp. 12-24. (P)

* C.P. Kindleberger, "The Case for Fixed Exchange Rates,1969," in The International Adjustment Mechanism, FRB of Boston, 1969, pp. 93-120. (P)

M. Friedman, "The Case for Fixed Exchange Rates," Essays in Positive Economics, 1953, pp. 157-203.

M. Friedman, Capitalism and Freedom, pp. 56-74.

M. Friedman, An Economist's Protest, Chapter 5.

A. Laffer, "Two Arguments For Fixed Rates," in Johnson and Swoboda, ed The Economics of Common Currencies, Chapter 1.

D. Baron, "Flexible Exchange Rates, Forward Markets, and the Level of Trade," American Economic Review, June 1976, pp. 253-66.

J. Wanniski, "The Mundell-Laffer Hypothesis...", The Public Interest, Spring 1975, pp. 31-52.

N. Fieleke, "The Worldwide Inflation," New England Economic Review, May/June 1976, pp. 3-29.

B. Optimal Currency Areas

* Y. Ishiyama, "Theory of Optimum Currency Areas: A Survey," IMF Staff Papers, July 1975.

* R. Mundell, "A Theory of Optimum Currency Areas," in Mundell, International Economics, Chapter 12.

* R. Mundell, "Uncommon Arguments for Common Currencies," in
  Johnson and Swoboda (eds.), <u>The Economics of Common Currencies</u>,
  Chapter 7.

J. Aschheim, "Artificial Currency Units: The Formation of Functional
  Currency Areas," Princeton Essays in International Finance,
  No. 114, April 1976.

C. <u>Monetary Independence</u>

R. Aliber, "Monetary Independence Under Floating Exchange Rates,"
  <u>Journal of Finance</u>, May 1975, pp. 365-376.

Meiselman and Laffer, ed., <u>The Phenomenon of Worldwide Inflation</u>,
  American Enterprise Institute, 1975. Especially papers by
  Haberler, Laffer, Meiselman, Mundell and Stein.

D. <u>International Liquidity, SDR and Seignorage</u>

B40.3383   Richard Levich
International Financial Markets   Spring 1981

Preliminary Lecture Schedule

Lecture #	Date	Topic
1	February 4	Introduction/Overview, balance of payments concepts and accounting
2	February 11	Building blocks, monetary exchange rate models
3	February 18	Rational expectations, exchange rate dynamics and overshooting
4	February 25	Foreign exchange market institutions, transaction cost and market maker behavior
5	March 4	Foreign exchange market efficiency--theory and evidence
6	March 11	Eurocurrencies--First principles, rate structure
7	March 18	Eurocurrencies-Policy
	March 25	Spring Recess
8	April 1	Forward exchange rate determination, forecasting
9	April 8	Foreign exchange risk pricing, stabilizing/destabilizing speculation
10	April 15	Government intervention, capital controls, European monetary system
11	April 22	Long-term capital flows, international portfolio diversification
12	April 29	International capital market theory
13	May 6	Macroeconomic policy-exchange rate systems
14	May 13	Macroeconomic policy-optimum currency area
	May 27	Final exam

Finance 394-3   Professor Stephen P. Magee
Spring, 1981   Department of Finance

INTERNATIONAL FINANCE

There are 3 required readings for this course:

1. Stephen P. Magee, International Trade, Addison-Wesley, 1980.
2. Eitman and Stonehill, Multinational Business Finance, 2nd. ed.,
   Addison-Wesley, 1979 (ES).
3. Donald Lessard, International Financial Management, Warren,
   Gorham and Lamont, 1979.

The first two items are textbooks and the third is a reading book.
The numbers in parentheses on this reading list are the chapter
numbers of the reading in the Lessard book.

Topic

1. INTERNATIONAL TRADE "Transport Costs; Trade in Standardized and
   New Products." Magee, chps. 1,2,3.

2. INTERNATIONAL TRADE "Raw Materials; Factors of Production and
   Policy." Magee, chps. 4,5,6.

3. EXCHANGE RATE DETERMINATION
   ES, chp. 2
   Ian Giddy, "An Integrated Theory of Exchange Rate Equilibrium,"
       JFQA, Dec. 1976 (13).
   Jacob Frenkel, "A Monetary Approach to the Exchange Rate,"
       Scandanavian Journal of Economics, May, 1976 (14).
   Rudiger Dornbusch, "Monetary Policy Under Exchange Rate Flexi-
       bility," in FRB of Boston, Managed Exchange Rate Flexi-
       bility, 1979 (15).
   Stephen P. Magee, "Empirical Evidence on the International
       Monetary Approach," American Economic Review 66 (May,
       1976), 163-170.

4. FOREIGN EXCHANGE EXPOSURE
   ES, chp. 3
   Richard Levich, "The Efficiency of Foreign Exchange Markets:
       A Review and Extension," in Dornbusch and Frenkel, Inter-
       national Economic Policy, 1979, (16).
   Frenkel and Levich, "Transaction Costs and Interest Arbitrage:
       Tranquil vs. Turbulent Periods," Journal of Political
       Economy, Nov., 1977 (17).
   Brad Cornell, "Spot Rates, Forward Rates and Market Efficiency,"
       JFE, 5-1977 (18).
   Stephen P. Magee, "Contracting and Spurious Deviations from
       Purchasing Power Parity," in Frenkel and Johnson, Studies
       in The Economics of Exchange Rates, 1978, chp. 4, 67-74.

5. FOREIGN EXCHANGE RISK
   ES, chp. 4
   Grauer, Litzenberger and Stehle, "Sharing Rules and Equilibrium in an International Capital Market Under Uncertainty: An Abridgement," JFE, 1976 (21)
   D. Logue and G. Oldfield, "Managing Foreign Assets When Foreign Exchange Markets are Efficient," Financial Management, 1977 (22).
   Ian Giddy, "Why It Doesn't Pay to Make a Habit of Forward Hedging," Euromoney, Dec., 1976, (23).
   R. Ankrom, "Top-Level Approach to Foreign Exchange Rate Problem," Harvard Business Review, July, 1974, (24).
   G. Dufey, "Corporate Finance and Exchange Rate Variations," Financial Management, Summer, 1972, (25).
   D. Heckerman, "The Exchange Risk of Foreign Operations," Journal of Business, Jan., 1972, (26).
   Stephen P. Magee, "A Two-Parameter Purchasing Power Measure of Arbitrage in International Goods Markets," in J. P. Martin and A. Smith, Trade and Payments Adjustment Under Flexible Exchange Rates. London: Macmillan, 1979, 152-173.
   Stephen P. Magee and Ramesh K. S. Rao, "Vehicle and Nonvehicle Currencies in International Trade," American Economic Review, May, 1980, 368-373.

6. INTERNATIONAL EQUITY MARKETS
   ES, chp. 5,6
   Richard Cooper, "Towards an International Capital Market?" in Kindleberger and Schonfield, North American and Western European Economic Policies, 1971 (6).
   Donald Lessard, "World, Country and Industry Relationships in Equity Returns," Fin. Analysts Journal, Jan., 1976 (7).
   R. Cohn and J. Pringle, "Imperfections in International Financial Markets," Journal of Finance, Mar., 1973, (8).
   Fischer Black, "International Capital Market Equilibrium with Investment Barriers, JFE, No. 1, 1974, (9).
   R. Stapleton and M. Subrahmanyam, "Market Imperfections, Capital Market Equilibrium and Corporate Finance," Journal of Finance, May, 1977 (10).
   R. Stehle, "An Emperical Test of ... National and International Pricing of Risky Assets," Journal of Finance, May, 1977, (11).
   B. Jacquillat and B. Solnik, "Multinationals are Poor Tools for Diversification," Journal of Portfolio Mgmt., Winter, 1978, (12).

REVIEW FOR MIDTERM EXAM BY TEACHING ASSISTANT

MIDTERM EXAM

7. LONG-RUN FOREIGN INVESTMENT
   ES, chp. 7
   Magee, Chp. 3

7. LONG-RUN FOREIGN INVESTMENT - continued

    C. P. Kindleberger, "The Theory of Foreign Investment," in _American Business Abroad_, 1969, chp. 1, (3)

    R. Vernon, "International Investment ... and Trade in the Product Cycle," _QJE_, 196

    G. Ragazzi, "Theories of The Determinants of Direct Foreign Investment," _IMF Staff Papers_, July, 1973 (4).

    Stephen P. Magee, "Information and the Multinational Corporation: An Appropriability Theory of Direct Foreign Investment," in J. Bhagwati, _The New International Economic Order_, MIT, 1977, (5).

8. THE EUROMARKETS
    ES, chp. 9
    Chp. 2, "The Determination of Eurocurrency Interest Rates," pp.48-86 in G. Dufey and I. Giddy, _The International Money Market_, PH, 1978.

9. THE COST OF CAPITAL AND FINANCIAL STRUCTURE
    ES, chp. 10
    S. Robins and R. Stobaugh, "Financing Foreign Affiliates," _Financial Mgmt._, Winter, 1973, (41).

    R. Naumann-Etienne, "A Framework for Financial Decisions in MNCs - A Summary of Recent Research," _JFQA_, Nov., 1974,(42).

10. MANAGEMENT OF WORKING CAPITAL
    ES, chps. 11,12
    A. Shapiro and D. Rutenberg, "Managing Exchange Risks in a Floating World," _Fin. Mgmt._,Summer 1976, (30).

    J. Makin, "Portfolio Theory and Foreign Exchange Risk," _JF_, May, 1978, (31).

    S. Lall, "Transfer Pricing by Multinational Manufacturing Firms," _Oxford Bull of Econ. & Stats._, Aug., 1973, (34).

    Stephen P. Magee, "Application of the Dynamic Limit Pricing Model to the Price of Technology and International Technology Transfer," in K. Brunner and A. Meltzer, _Optimal Policies, Control Theory and Technology Exports_, North-Holland, 1977, 203-224.

    D. Rutenberg, "Maneuvering Liquid Assets in MNC ..." _Mgmt Science_, June, 1970.

11. INTERNATIONAL BANKING
    ES, Chps. 13,14.

    HOLIDAY

12. ACCOUNTING, CONTROL AND TAXATION
    ES, chp. 15,16
    E. Fredrikson, "On The Measurement of Foreign Income," _J. of Accounting Res._, Aug., 1968, (27).

    R. Aliber and C. Stickney, "Accounting Measures for Foreign Exchange Exposure: the Long and Short of It," _Accting. Rev._, Jan. 1973, (28).

    J. Shank, "FASB Statement of Resolved Foreign Currency Accounting - Or Did It?" _Fin. Analysts Journ._, July, 1976,(29).

    S. Robbins and R. Stobaugh, "The Bent Measuring Stick for Foreign Subsidiaries," _Harvard Business Review_, Sept. 1973, (37).

12. ACCOUNTING, CONTROL AND TAXATION - continued

   D. Lessard and P. Lorange, "Currency Changes and Management Control ...," Accting. Rev., July, 1977 (38).

   A. Shapiro, "Capital Budgeting for the MNC," Fin. Mgmt., Spring, 1978 (39).

   D. Lessard, "Evaluating Foreign Projects: An Adjusted Present Value Approach" (40).

   T. Horst, "American Taxation of Multinational Firms," AER, June, 1977, (35).

REVIEW FOR FINAL EXAM

FINAL EXAMS

New York University
Graduate School of Business Administration

B40.3385
International Corporation Finance

Professor Rita M. Maldonado-Bear
Spring 1981

SYLLABUS
# # # # # #

Objective

The objective of this course is to examine (1) the investment,
(2) the financing and (3) the working capital management processes of
a multinational firm within the context of market imperfection, foreign
exchange risk, political risk, inflation, tax laws and accounting regu-
lations. Within a theoretical frame, the course will emphasize a practi-
cal approach.

Prerequisites

A basic understanding of the theory of corporation finance and
international economics and finance is necessary. Therefore, the
courses B05.2312 Problems in Financial Management and B40.2381 International Trade and Finance are required. It is strongly recommended
that B40.3383 International Financial Markets is taken prior to or con-
currently with this course.

Assignments and Examinations

Class sessions will be devoted to discussion of the topics presented in the course outline, four cases that are assigned, and several
selected problems or exercises. It is required that, in advance of each
lecture, the student read thoroughly all the assigned readings and prepare all other assignments pertaining to the topic under discussion.

The class will be divided into groups and each group will be
responsible for a thorough analysis of each case. The cases are to be
typewritten (see instructions on page 7 of this syllabus) and handed in
at the beginning of the class, during which they will be discussed as
per course outline.

The problems and exercises, which are to be done individually,
should also be handed in the date that they are due, as per course
outline. Even though these will not be graded there will be a 5% deduc-
tion from the final grade for each assignment not handed in.

There will be a mid-term and a final, and the course grade will be
determined as follows:

4 cases	20%	
Mid-term	30%	
Final	50%	
Several Exercises & Problems	-5% per assignment if not handed in	

Required Materials

David K. Eitman and Arthur F. Stonehill, <u>Multinational Business
Finance</u>, Second Edition, (Addison-Wesley, 1979). [E&S]

A package of cases available at the Bookstore.

Donald R. Lessard (Ed.), <u>International Financial Management
Theory and Application</u>, (Warren, Gorham & Lamont, 1979). Several
articles from this book are recommended reading, only a few are
required reading. Several copies are available on reserve at our
library and therefore you do not need to buy the book. [L]

Recommended: Texts

Rita Rodriguez and Eugene Carter, <u>International Financial Manage-
ment</u>, (Prentice Hall, 1979).

J. Fred Weston and Bart W. Sage, <u>Guide to International Financial
Management</u>, (McGraw Hill, 1977).

Recommended:

Other Publications of interest to those who want to become very
familiar and stay up-to-date in international financial management:

A. Publications that contain economic and financial statistics
for different countries, all available in our GBA Library:

1. <u>IMF International Financial Statistics</u>, Monthly.

2. <u>International Economic Indicators</u>, Quarterly. It include
almost all relevant economic and financial variables for
industrialized countries. It does not include interest
rates. <u>U.S. Department of Commerce</u>.

3. <u>OECD Economic Outlook</u>, Bi-annual. Contains country by
country (16 European, U.S., Canada and Japan) evaluation
and annual data on Gross Domestic Product, Consumer Pric
Index, Current Account Balance,Nominal Exchange Rates.

4. <u>OECD Financial Statistics</u>, Issued yearly with five per-
iodic supplements, and monthly updating interest rates.
A unique collection of data of financial markets in 16
European countries, the United States, Canada, and Japan
Comparable data only for GDP and Money Supply.

5. <u>OECD Main Economic Indicators</u>, Monthly publication of th
organization for Economic Cooperation and Development
(OECD). A tabulation of international indicators of
economic activity. It has interest rates, money supply,
Consumer Price Index, GNP deflator, international reserv
in SDR's,unemployment, GNP, etc.

B. Publications containing current events in the international
   environment.

   1. <u>Business International Money Report</u>. Business Inter-
      national. Expensive ($250), but good weekly survey of
      business practice. (GBA Library, reference--8th floor).

   2. <u>Euromoney</u>. A monthly British publication that has
      excellent short articles by leading members of the
      financial community. (GBA Library, Periodical--7th
      floor).

   3. <u>Financing Foreign Operations</u>. Business International.
      Expensive ($250 p.a.), monthly update on financing alter-
      natives in all the major world financial centers. Most
      large companies subscribe so check your firm's library.
      (GBA Library, Reference--8th floor).

   4. <u>Financial Management</u>. More theoretical than Euromoney.
      Published quarterly. (GBA Library, Periodicals--7th
      floor).

   5. <u>IMF Survey</u>, Monthly publication by International Mone-
      tary Fund. Available in our library.

   6. <u>The International Tax Report</u>. A bi-weekly publication
      from the Institute of International Research Ltd. Expen-
      sive ($120 p.a.), but is useful for anyone who wishes to
      keep abreast of the changing tax negotiations as they
      affect the multinational corporation. (Not in our GBA
      Library, but check your firm's library).

   7. <u>World Financial Markets</u>. Morgan Guaranty Trust of New
      York. Sent to international treasurers of companies who
      are clients of the above bank. Basically a good economic
      analysis of the changing conditions in the money market.
      (GBA Library, Periodicals--7th floor).

<u>Office Hours for Students</u>

I will be available to see you or talk to you on the telephone
<u>during my office hours for students</u> in my office, Room 1110, Merrill
Hall.

    Telephone No.: 285-6160
    Hours: Monday   3:00 - 6:00 p.m.
               Wednesday 10:00 -11:00 a.m.

COURSE OUTLINE
# # # # # # # #

1 & 2   Introduction and Balance of Payments Review

Required assignment:
1)   E & S Chapter 1

Recommended assignment:
1)   Donald S. Kemp, "Balance of Payments Concepts –
      What Do They Really Mean?" Monthly Review, Federal
      Reserve Bank of St. Louis, July 1975.
2)   R. Maldonado, "Recording and Classifying Transactions
      in the Balance of Payments", Journal of International
      Accounting, forthcoming Fall 1979. Available in
      manuscript form at reserve room in library.

3   Interrelationship of Exchange Rates, Prices and Interest Rates

Required assignment:
1)   E & S Chapter 2
2)   Foreign exchange exercises, pp. 70-72 in E&S
3)   Balance of Payments exercise distributed in class.

Recommended assignment:
1)   Ian H. Giddy, "An Integrated Theory of Exchange
      Rate Equilibrium", in L p. 167.
2)   Henry C. Wallich, "What Makes Exchange Rates Move",
      Challenge, July-August, 1977.
3)   Stephen H. Goodman, "Foreign Exchange Rate Fore-
      casting Techniques: Implications for Business and
      Policy," Journal of Finance, May 1979.
4)   Thomas M. Humphrey, "The Purchasing Power Parity
      Doctrine," Economic Review, FRB of Richmond,
      June 1979.
5)   Gunter Dufey and Ian Giddy, "Forecasting Exchange
      Rates in a Floating World," Euromoney, Nov. 1975,
      pp. 28-35.

4   Foreign Exchange Exposure

Required assignment:
1)   E & S Chapter 3
2)   John K. Shank, "FASB Statement 8 Resolved Foreign
      Currency Accounting-Or Did It?" in L p. 435.
3)   CASE - The Mexican Peso.

Recommended assignment:
1)   Aliber & Sickney, "Accounting Measures for Foreign
      Exchange Exposure: The Long and Short of It",
      in L p. 425.

2)   Evans, Folks and Jilling, <u>The Impact of Statement</u>
<u>of Financial Accounting Standards No. 8 on the</u>
<u>Foreign Exchange Risk Management Practices of</u>
<u>American Multinationals</u>, Financial Accounting
Standards Board, Nov. 1978.

5   <u>Reacting to Foreign Exchange Exposure</u>

Required assignment:

1)   E & S Chapter 4
2)   Sierra, Marquez and Sumac, problems in E&S,
pp. 150 & 151.
3)   CASE - The Delta L1011

Recommended assignment:

1)   Giddy, "Why It Doesn't Pay to Make a Habit of
Forward Hedging", in L p. 375.
2)   Duffy, "Corporate Finance and Exchange Rate
Variations", in L p. 391
3)   Fieleke, "Foreign Exchange Speculation by US Firms:
Some New Evidence", <u>New England Economic Review</u>,
FRB of Boston, March-April 1979.

6   <u>Political and Country Risk</u>

Required assignment:

1)   E & S Chapters 5 & 6
2)   Notes on measuring Foreign Investment Risk in
Cases package.
3)   Protection against Political Upheaval, New York
Times, 1979, in Cases package.

Recommended assignment:

1)   Saigen, "Economic Indicators and Country Risk
Appraisal", <u>Economic Review</u>, FRB of San Francisco,
Fall 1977.
2)   Rummel & Heenan, "How Multinationals Analyze
Political Risk", <u>Harvard Business Review</u>, January-
February 1978.
3)   Haendel, West & Meadow, "Overseas Investment and
Political Risk", Philadelphia: Foreign Policy
Research Institute Monograph Series #21, 1975.
4)   Knudsen, "Explaining the National Propensity to
Expropriate: An Ecological Approach", <u>Journal of</u>
<u>International Business Studies</u>, Spring 1974.

7   MID-TERM

8 & 9   <u>International Capital Budgeting</u>

Required assignment:

1)   E & S Chapters 7 & 8
2)   Shapiro, "Capital Budgeting for the Multinational
Corporation", in L p. 567

3)   CASE - Chaolandia's Super-Widgets

Recommended assignment:

1)   Ragazzi, "Theories of the Determinants of Direct
     Foreign Investment", in L p. 31.
2)   Solnick, "Why Not Diversify Internationally Rather
     Than Domestically?" in L p. 13.
3)   Jacquillat & Solnick, "Multinationals are Poor
     Tools for Diversification", in L p. 157.

10, 11   Capital Markets and the Cost of Capital

Required assignment:

1)   E & S Chapters 9 & 10 and Appendix A & B
2)   Lessard, "Evaluating Foreign Projects:and Adjusted
     Present Value Approach", in L p. 577.
3)   Robicheck & Eaker, "Debt Denominations and Exchange
     Risk in International Markets", Financial Management,
     Autumn 1976.
4)   CASE

Recommended assignment:

1)   Duffy-Giddy, The International Money Market,
     (Prentice-Hall, Inc. 1978).
2)   Shapiro, "Financial Structure and Cost of Capital in
     a Multinational Corporation", Journal of Financial
     and Quantitative Analysis, June 1978.

12, 13   Working Capital Management

Required assignment:

1)   E & S Chapters 11, 12, 13
2)   E&S Problems, p. 530-North Crawley Equipment and
                    p. 532-Pfusterschmidt, GMBH

Recommended assignment:

1)   Shapiro, "Evaluating Financing Costs for Multi-
     national Subsidiaries", in L p. 475.
2)   Shapiro & Rutenberg, "Managing Exchange Risk in a
     Floating World", in L p. 443.
3)   Barrett, "Case of the Tangled Transfer Price",
     in L p. 485.
4)   Lall, "Transfer-Pricing by Multinational Manufactur-
     ing Firms", in L p. 495.

14   Accounting Control and Taxation

Required assignment:

1)   E & S Chapters 15 & 16.
2)   Lessard & Lorange, "Currency Changes and Management
     Control: Resolving the Centralization/Decentrali-
     zation Dilemma", in L p. 555.

INSTRUCTIONS FOR CASE PRESENTATION

1.   A case should <u>never exceed 5</u> double spaced typewritten pages
      of text plus appendix where relevant.

2.   The case should be organized in the following form:

      A.   Introduction - A paragraph where the problem is introduced.

      B.   The general approach to the solution should be organized,
            original and should include:

            a)   facts and assumptions
            b)   accurate computations which can vary with the assump-
                 tions made. The summary of computations may appear
                 in the text. Lengthy computations, tables, graphs, etc.
                 should appear in appendix.

      C.   Conclusion which should be:

            a)   correct or accurate
            b)   relevant to the material presented in B) and the
                 assumptions made.

3.   The typewritten case (1 per group) should be handed in at the
      beginning of the class the day that the case is due.

4.   Please write your group number as well as the names of all
      group members on the front page of your typewritten case.

DALHOUSIE UNIVERSITY
School of Business Administration

MBA 696A   International   Dr. Alan M. Rugman
Finance   Fall, 1981

Introduction of Course Themes

     The focus of this course is the international banking and financial markets
of Canada and its relationships with major international financial centres.
The structure and operations of these markets will be examined and relevant
institutional aspects will be highlighted. Then the impact of the markets on
traders, investors, bankers, and the managers of both domestic and multinational
corporations is explored. The special feature of the course is its development
of a modern theoretical model of the foreign exchange markets of Canada and the
consistent application of this model throughout the course to explain the
management of foreign exchange risk and exposure.

     International trade and foreign direct investment have always been of
great importance in an open economy such as Canada but it is only recently
that the role of the multinational enterprise has been recognized and its impact
studied. The role of the multinational as a vehicle for international
diversification in a world of imperfect markets has also been studied recently.
This course builds upon such work on the internal markets of multinationals
and explores the consequences of foreign exchange risk for multinationals
in Canada as well as the growing number of multinationals based in Canada. The
management of foreign exchange risk is considered in two ways; at a macro and
at a micro level. The two levels are clearly interrelated but, whenever possible,
they are separated for pedagogical purposes.

     The micro part of the course starts with the development of an integrated
model of the foreign exchange market in a Canadian context. It explains the
interest rate parity theorem (IRP), the purchasing power parity theorem (PPP)
and the international Fisher effect (IFE) and then integrates these concepts
in an attempt to explain Canadian foreign exchange relationships. It then
examines empirical studies of this model using Canadian data and contrasts
experience with theory. This new paradigm of the foreign exchange market has
attracted considerable professional attention over the last ten years but its
implications have not been worked out for Canadian students. This course
fills the gap.

     Once the theoretical basis of the course has been established its implications
are fully explored for the management of foreign exchange risk by managers of
firms active in international trade and investments. The role of foreign exchange
risk and the exposure of multinationals and domestic firms is explored. Data
are analyzed on the performance of both Canadian based multinationals and also
the effects of foreign exchange risk on the performance of multinationals in
Canada. The organization design of the financial function of a multinational
is discussed. The appropriate cost of capital is worked out for a firm faced
with foreign exchange risk. Reasons for transfer pricing are analyzed.

     The macro part of the course examines the nature and structure of
international financial markets in Canada. It does so in the context of the

theory of foreign exchange, thus it explains the difference between spot and forward foreign exchange rates (which exist with certainty) and the expected future spot rate (which is not known). It asks whether the forward exchange rate is an unbiased predictor of the expected future spot rate and if so, what is the role of forecasting? It analyzes the efficiency of the foreign exchange market and its interrelationship with domestic and foreign debt and equity markets.

A major section of the course develops an explanation of the reasons for growth of the Eurocurrency market and relates this to the recent developments of offshore banking activity by the large Canadian chartered banks. The increasing degree of multinational activity by Canadian banks is explained and related to tests of the profitability of the industry. Also considered are the implications of foreign bank entry into the previously protected Canadian banking sector. The effect of this outside competition on the international banking services of Canadian banks is discussed. The course concludes both a reappraisal of the U.S. and Canadian financial markets and considers the degree of integration of these markets in the light of increased activities by both U.S. and Canadian based multinational enterprises and banks.

The Text Books

All texts are written for the U.S. market; none focus exclusively (indeed, few even discuss) Canada.

Required text :

Eiteman and Stonehill. Multinational Business Finance (Addison-Wesley, 2nd edn., 1979).

Recommended texts:

E. Carter and R. Rodriguez. International Financial Management (Prentice Hall, 2 edn., 1979).

Donald R. Lessard (ed.). International Financial Management (Boston: Warren, Gorham and Lamont, 1979).

David B. Zenoff and J. Zwick. International Financial Management (New York: Prentice Hall, 1969).

Case Book: (Required)

Carlson, Robert S. et al. International Finance: Cases (Addison-Wesley)

Other relevant books: (Recommended)

Alan M. Rugman. International Diversification and the Multinational Enterprise (Lexington: D.C. Heath, 1979).

Gunter Dufey and Ian H. Giddy. The International Money Market (Prentice Hall, 1978).

Other texts:

Robert Z. Aliber. Exchange Risk and Corporate International Finance (Halsted
     Press, 1978).

Ronald I. McKinnon. Money in International Exchange (Oxford University Press,
     1979).

Sidney M. Robbins and Robert B. Stobaugh. Money in the Multinational Enterprise
     (New York: Basic Books, 1973).

Charles N. Henning, W. Pigott and R.H. Scott. International Financial Management
     (New York: McGraw-Hill, 1978).

Yoshi Tsurumi. Multinational Management (Ballinger Press, 1977).

David A. Ricks. International Dimensions of Corporate Finance (Prentice-Hall,
     1978).

Raj Aggarwal. Financial Policies for the Multinational Company (New York:
     Praeger, 1976).

Edwin J. Elton and Martin J. Gruber (eds.). International Capital Markets
     (Amsterdam: North-Holland, 1975).

Bruno H. Solnik. European Capital Markets: Towards a General Theory of
     International Investment (Lexington, Mass.: Lexington Books, 1973).

Texts on International Monetary Economics (Reference):

Robert Z. Aliber. The International Money Game (New York: Basic Books, 1973
     and 1977).

William M. Scammell. International Monetary Policy: Bretton Woods and After
     (London: Macmillan, 1975).

H. Robert Heller. International Monetary Economics (Prentice-Hall, 1974).

Robert A. Mundell. International Economics (Macmillan, 1968).

Robert A. Mundell. Monetary Theory (Goodyear, 1971).

John Williamson. The Failure of World Monetary Reform, 1971-74 (Nelson, 1977).

Jacob A. Frenkel and Harry G. Johnson. The Monetary Approach to the Balance
     of Payments.

Jacob A. Frenkel and Harry G. Johnson. The Economics of Exchange Rates:
     Selected Studies (Addison-Wesley, 1978).

Carl H. Stem, John H. Makin and Dennis E. Logue. Eurocurrencies and the
     International Monetary System (Washington, D.C.: American Enterprise
     Institute, 1976).

Recent Bibliographies of International Business and Finance:

Michael Z. Brooke et al. (eds.). A Bibliography of International Business (London: Macmillan, 1977).

Virod B. Bavishi et al. (eds.). International Financial Management: Survey and Bibliography 1973-1976 (Ohio State University College of Administrative Science Working Paper No. 77-22, June 1977).

Sanjaya Lall. Foreign Private Manufacturing Investment and Multinational Corporations: An Annotated Bibliography (New York: Praeger, 1975).

Raj Aggarwal. International Business Finance: An Annotated Bibliography (New York: Praeger, 1979).

Journals with Specialization in International Business and Finance:

Columbia Journal of World Business
California Management Review
Journal of World Trade Law

More Technical Journals:

Journal of International Business Studies
Weltwirtschaftliches Archiv (Journal of World Economics)
Journal of International Economics
Management International Review
The Economic Journal
Journal of Finance
Journal of Business
Journal of Financial and Quantitative Analysis
Financial Analysts Journal

ASSIGNMENTS AND GRADES

The method of instruction for this advanced course will combine lectures with seminars and case discussion. Class participation is required in the latter. Each student will be required to give at least one seminar presentation or case study. For this (s)he should prepare a brief written paper. Another piece of written work will be required in the form of a term paper. (If the class size exceeds 30 then case discussion may be replaced by a paper.) There will be a final examination.

DISTRIBUTION OF GRADES

Class and case participation	30%
Term paper	30%
Final examination	40%
	100%

Detailed Outline of Course Contents

Date	Week No.	Topic
16 Sept.	1	Introduction: Canada as an open economy; Canadian balance of payments and capital flows; the firm in and international setting.
23 Sept.	2	The Foreign Exchange Market in Canada: The currency factor; international aspects of Canada's foreign exchange market; tables of foreign exchange rates, cross rates; spot, forward and future exchange rates, their determination and meaning; possibilities for speculation and arbitrage; is hedging relevant? Other major international financial centres.
30 Sept.	3	An Integrated Model of the Foreign Exchange Market: Interest Rate Parity (IRP); Purchasing Power Parity (PPP); International Fisher Effect (IFE); interrelationships of IRP, PPP and IFE.
7 Oct.	4	The Efficiency of Foreign Exchange Markets: Data on Canadian exchange and capital markets; integration of U.S. and Canadian exchange and equity markets; forecasting exchange rates, economic, political factors and transaction costs; exchange risk and asset valuation.
14 Oct.	5	The Management of Exchange Risk by Multinationals: Foreign exchange risk and exposure; methods of exchange risk protection; accounting, translation and economic exposure; FAS Standard No. 8 and its revisions, Canadian accounting standards; multinational working capital management.
21 Oct.	6	IN RESERVE
28 Oct.	7	International Diversification: By individuals under perfect markets; by multinationals under imperfect markets; theory of internalization, international corporate asset valuation.
4 Nov.	8	Asset Investment and Financing for Multinationals: Cost of capital for multinationals; capital budgeting evaluations, techniques and practices; transfer pricing and taxes; centralized finance function for multinationals; import and export financing, letters of credit.
11 Nov.	9	REMEMBERANCE DAY - HOLIDAY
18 Nov.	10	The International Financial Markets: The international monetary system after Bretton Woods; adjustment mechanisms under fixed and flexible rates; the monetary approach to the balance of payments and its implications for corporate international finance.

25 Nov.	11	The Eurocurrency Market: Reasons for its development; imperfections in U.S. regulated system of financial intermediation; efficiency of the unregulated Eurocurrency market; the Eurobond market; international currency diversification.
2 Dec.	12	Canadian Multinational Banking: Multinational banking – role and significance for international business; reasons for increase in offshore banking in Canada; increase in foreign assets and relationships to profitability; Bank Act revision of 1980 and the entry of foreign banks to Canada; recent developments in international banking services.
9 Dec.	13	Conclusions: The integration of U.S. and Canadian financial markets.

NORTHWESTERN UNIVERSITY

J.L. KELLOGG GRADUATE SCHOOL OF MANAGEMENT

FINANCE D70

INTERNATIONAL FINANCE

Lemma W. Senbet   Spring 1981

Office: 5-104 Leverone Hall

Finance D70 is a broad survey of international financial principles
underlying the investment and financing decisions of multinatinational firms
and international investors. A survey of the major macro-economic factors
bearing on the international corporate financial decisions are provided in
Section II. Section III deals with the determinants of capital flows across
national boundaries in the context of international portfolio theories. Section
IV, which considers foreign exchange transactions and hedging strategies, is
the most important element of the course. Consequently, 2 to 3 weeks will be
devoted to this section. Sections V and VI look at multinational long-term
investment and long-term financing decisions. In particular, these sections
examine special adjustments of capital budgeting and capital structure decisions
for the international setting. The balance of the course surveys the characteristics of the international financial markets (with emphasis on Eurocurrency
markets), international taxation, and special topics (depending upon the availability of time). The reading list for the special topics will be announced later.

COURSE OUTLINE AND READING LIST

Required Texts:

Rita Rodriquez and E. Eugene Carter. Internat.ional Financial Management
(Englewood Cliffs, N.J.: Prentice-Hall, 1979). [Referred in the Reading
List as "Text".].

Robert Aliber. The International Money Game (Basic Books, 1976).

The texts are supplemented by journal articles in the case packet.

Recommended (Library Reserve):

Franklin Root. International Trade and Investment (South-Western
Publishing Co., 1978).

You should also acquaint yourself with the following vital sources of
current international data:

1. International Financial Statistics (The International Monetary Fund)
2. Capital International Perspective (Chase World Information)
3. World Financial Markets (Morgan Guaranty Trust Co.)
4. Survey of Current Business (U.S. Department of Commerce)
5. The Wall Street Journal
6. Journal of Commerce, Etc.

I. Introduction

A. Course Objectives
B. Multinational Business Finance: Overview

II. International Financial Environment

A. The Balance of International Payments
   Text: Chapters 2,3,4 (pp. 69-78)
   "Report of the Advisory Committee on the Presentation of
   Balance of Payments Statistics," Survey of Current Business,
   (June, 1976).

   Exercises on Balance of Payments Accounting, p.28 (Text)

B. A Sketch of International Monetary Arrangements: History and Current
   Status

   Aliber: Chapters 3, 4, 6, 19
   Text: Chapter 4 (pp. 78-102)
   Root: Chapter 17*

C. The Foreign Exchange Market

   Text: Chapter 5 (pp. 119-133)
   Root: Chapter 11
   Aliber: Chapter 2

   Exercise: Answer question 2 (Chapter 5: Text)

E. The International Financial Environment and the Oil Problem. Arthur
   Laffer (1974). "The Balance of Payments and Exchange-Rate Systems,"
   Financial Analysts Journal (July-August).

   "The OPEC Surplus and Financial Flows in 1975," World Financial Markets
   (Morgan Guaranty Trust Co., October 1975). Also see the issues for
   Sept.-Dec., 1976.

---
*
Optional

III. Determinants of International Capital Flows
       Root: Chapter 22*

Haim Levy and Marshal Sarnat (1970). "International Diversification
   of Investment Portfolios," American Economic Review (September),
   pp. 668-675.

Donald Heckerman (1973). "On the Effects of Exchange Risk," Journal
   of International Economics, 3, pp. 379-387.

Georgio Ragazzi (1973). "Theories of the Determinants of Direct Foreign
   Investment," IMF Staff Papers (July), pp. 471-498.

John Dunning (1973). "The Determinants of International Production,"
   Oxford Economic Papers (November).

Bruno Solnik (1974). "Why Not Diversify Internationally Rather Than
   Domestically?" Financial Analysts Journal (July-August), pp. 48-54.

Tamir Agmon and Donald Lessard (1977). "Investor Recognition of Corporate
   International Diversification," Journal of Finance (September),
   pp. 1049-1055.

Bertrand Jacquillat and Bruno H. Solnik (1978). "Multinationals are Poor
   Tools for Diversification" Journal of Portfolio Management (Winter) pp. 8-

Vihang R. Errunza and Lemma W. Senbet (1981). "The Effects of International
   Operations on the Market Value of the Firm: Theory and Evidence",
   forthcoming, Journal of Finance [May].

IV. Foreign Exchange Transactions and Hedging Strategies

    A. Arbitrage, Speculation and Forward Rate Determination
          Text: Chapter 5, pp. 133-151. Answer question 3.

       Robert Aliber (1973). "The Interest Rate Parity Theorem:
       A Reinterpretation," Journal of Political Economy (December),
       pp. 1451-59.

       Martin Murenbeeld (1975). "Economic Factors for Forecasting Foreign
       Exchange Rate Changes," Columbia Journal of World Business (Summer)

    B. Foreign Exchange Risk and Protective Strategies
          Text: Chapters 6-8. Answer question 1 (Chapter 7).

       Alan Shapiro (1977). "Defining Exchange Risk," Journal of Business
       (January), pp. 37-39.
       Discussion of FASB #8 and the new exposure draft
       John Shank (1976), "FASB Statement 8 Resolved Foreign Currency
       Accounting-Or Did It?" Financial Analysts Journal (July-August) pp.

* Optional

C. Overall Management of Foreign Exchange Position (International Working Capital Management)
   Text: Chapter 9

   Rita Rodriguez (1978). "Management of Foreign Exchange Risk in U.S. Multinationals," Sloan Management Review (Spring).

   Alan Shapiro and David Rutenberg (1976). "Managing Exchange Risks in a Floating World," Financial Management (Summer), pp. 48-58.

   Answer question 7 (Chapter 9: Text)

V. Evaluation of Direct Foreign Investments

   A. The Scope of the Multinational Enterprise
      Text: Chapter 12
      Root: Chapter 21
      Aliber: Chapter 16

   B. The Foreign Investment Decision
      Case: Chaolandia Super Widgets

      1. Cash Flow Analysis
         Text: Chapter 10, pp. 369-383, 322-3.

      2. International Risk Dimensions and Multinational Capital Budgeting
         Text: Chapter 10, pp. 382-394, Chapters 11, 13. Handout Problems.

         Donald Lessard (1979) "Evaluating Foreign Projects: An Adjusted Present Value Approach." International Financial Management by Donald Lessard.

VI. International Corporate Long-Term Financing Decisions

    Arthur Stonehill and Thomas Stitzel (1969). "Financial Structure and Multinational Corporation," California Management Review (Fall), pp. 39-54.

    Alan Shapiro (1975). "Evaluating Financing Costs for Multinational Subsidiaries," Journal of International Business Studies (Fall).

    Lemma Senbet (1979). "International Capital Market Equilibrium and the Multinational Firm Financing and Investment Policies," Journal of Financial and Quantitative Analysis, (September), pp. 455-480.

    Alan Shapiro (1978). "Financial Structure and Cost of Capital in the Multinational Corporation," JFQA (June).

VII. International Financial Markets

     Text: Chapters 14-16
     Aliber: Chapters 7,17

     Milton Friedman (1969). "The Euro-dollar Market: Some First Principles," The Morgan Guaranty Survey (October).

Robert Aliber (1977). "The Integration of the Offshore and Domestic Banking System," Unpublished Manuscript.

VIIII. Taxation of International Business

Text: Appendix One
Aliber: Chapter 12

Mitsuo Sato and Richard Bird (1975).* "International Aspects of the Taxation of Corporations and Shareholders," The IMF Staff Papers (July)

IX. Special Topics

A. Financial Reporting of International Operations.
B. International Mutual Fund Performance Evaluation.
C. Recent Developments in International Banking.

GRADING

The overall grade will be determined on the basis of:

MIDTERM EXAM and/or Case Analysis
FINAL EXAM
Graded Assignments, if any

A term paper may serve as a substitute for a case analysis, and it may be satisfied by anyone of the following:
1) A critique of an article on an important topic.
2) A research project.
3) A critical literature review of a significant subject matter.

The assignments listed in the outline are for class discussion, but some may be collected and graded without prior announcement.

New York University

Graduate School of Business Administration

B40.3387   Spring 1981
International Banking   Prof. I. Walter
Mondays, 7:25-9:10 P.M.   Merrill Hall

This course is intended to serve as an introduction to international banking. It begins with a brief discussion of the international banking environment--the importance of factors affecting international trade, monetary relations, corporate finance and financial markets. Substantial emphasis is placed on country risk assessment, including a simulation exercise that provides the framework for this part of the course.

Also included toward the end of the course are sessions on legal aspects of international lending, project financing and regulatory issues facing international banks. The theory of multinational corporations is applied to the banking sector in an attempt to determine sources of competitive strength, market share, profitability, growth and similar dimensions of performance by international banks in the marketplace. Factors affecting top management decisions on whether and how to service international markets, and the implications for the structure of the bank itself, are examined through case analyses. Case discussions are employed to develop principles of international project financing, credit analysis, evaluation of foreign banks and establishment of correspondent networks, and analysis of country conditions that may affect international bank and non-bank relationships.

Prerequisites: Students registering for this course should have had previous courses in basic economics, accounting and financial analysis at the undergraduate or graduate level.

Pedagogy: The course is case-oriented, allowing students to apply principles developed in class to actual international banking situations. A two-page written brief is required for each case. A term project will involve developing international banking strategies for 5 banks, with students working in groups of 10.

Readings: There is no good textbook available on international banking. Extensive reading assignments are made from two specialized books:

> T.H. Donaldson, <u>Lending in International Commercial Banking</u>
> (London: Macmillan, 1979).

> Steven I. Davis, <u>The Management Function in International Banking</u>
> (London: Macmillan, 1979).

Because both of these books are expensive, several copies will be kept on library reserve for this course, and students who cannot afford to purchase them should read the assignments in the library. Five cases, as specified below, are available for purchase from the bookstore which contain a variety of assigned articles. Additional material may be distributed to students during the semester. Students are requested to have read the assignments <u>before</u> coming to class.

The Environment of International Banking

1. What international banking is all about
2. Relationships of domestic and international banking
3. The international commercial and financial environment
4. Relevant developments in international financial markets
5. The legal environment

Readings: Davis, Chapters 1-3; Harvard Business School, "An Introduction to Commerical Banks" (xeroxed); John P. Segala, "A Summary of the International Banking Act of 1978" (xeroxed).

Session 2   Monday, 9 February 1981

The Theory of Multinational Banking

1. Review of the theory of multinational enterprise
2. Application to international banking
3. Criteria of competitiveness
4. Price and non-price competitive variables
5. Measures and determinants of performance

Readings: Davis, Chapter 4; Herbert G. Grubel, "A Theory of Multinational Banking" (xeroxed); H. Peter Gray and Jean M. Gray, "The International Bank: A Financial MNC?"

Session 3   Monday, 23 February 1981

On Going International

1. Managerial objectives
2. What are the alternatives?
3. Criteria for assessing alternatives
4. Comparative evaluation of options
5. The decision process

Readings: Davis, Chapters 5-7.

Case: Lincoln National Bank (ICCH 4-273-040).

Session 4   Monday 23 February 1981

Risks and Returns in International Banking

1. Measuring exposure to and assignment of risk
2. Lender objective functions
2. Problems of liability management
3. Letters of credit
4. Composite loss functions
5. Pathology of problem situations
6. Country scenarios

Readings: Donaldson, Chapter 3; Euromoney, "Erwin Blumenthal is Zaire's Last Hope" (xeroxed); Euromoney, "El Dorado: A Lesson in Loan Negotiating" (xeroxed); R. Chernow, "The IMF: Roughest Bank in Town" (xeroxed).

<u>Session 5</u>   Monday, 2 March 1981

<u>Sources of Country Risk: Structural and Monetary Elements</u>

1. Patterns of growth and economic structure
2. Forecasting the sources of growth
3. The banking and financial sector and exchange rates
4. The quality of economic management
5. Selecting leading indicators

Readings: Donaldson, Chapter 8; Robert Z. Aliber, "Living with Developing Country Debt: (xeroxed); Ingo Walter, "International Capital Allocation".

<u>Session 6</u>   Monday 9 March 1981

<u>Sources of Country Risk: Balance of Payments</u>

1. Shifting competitive advantage
2. Diversification and risk in international trade
3. Foreign direct investment flows
4. Access to debt markets and refinancings
5. Analysis of size and structure of external debt

Readings: Donaldson, Chapter 9; K. Saini and P. Bates, "Statistical Techniques for Determining Debt-Servicing Capacity for Developing Countries" (xeroxed); Arturo C. Porzecanski, "The Assessment of Country Risk: Lessons from the Latin American Experience" (xeroxed).

<u>Session 7</u>   Monday 16 March 1981

<u>Country Risk: Political Dimensions and Systems Design</u>

1. Sources of internal political risk
2. Sources of external political risk
3. Political overlay of economic policy
4. Problems of estimator bias
5. Applications of country risk assessment
6. Design of international exposure management systems

Readings: Donaldson, Chapter 10; Stephen J. Kobrin, "Political Risk: A Review and Reconsideration" (xeroxed); R. Puz, "How to Find Out When a Sovereign Borrower Slips from A-1 to C-3" (xeroxed).

<u>Case:</u> Schubert National Bank (ICCH 9-280-600).

Session 8   Monday, 30 March 1981

Project Financing and Loan Syndication

1. The nature of project financing
2. Project analysis
3. Assembling a syndicate
4. Questions of pricing and returns
5. Cofinancing

Readings: Donaldson, Chapters 4 and 5.

Case: Cook Country Trust Co. (ICCH 4-277-178).

Session 9   Monday, 6 April 1981

Analysis of International Credits

1. Principles of international credit analysis and trade financing
2. International versus domestic credits
3. Currency and cash flow analysis
4. Balance sheet analysis
5. Lending to foreign affiliates of domestic firms

Readings: Donaldson, Chapters 2 and 6.

Case: Ampro Europe

Session 10   Monday, 13 April 1981

International Merchant Banking

1. Direct placements
2. International and Euro bond underwritings
3. Mergers and acquisitions
4. Multinational corporate advisory series
5. Country advisory series

Readings: S.M. Yassukovich, The Techniques of International Investment Banking
(London: Macmillan, 1980), selected chapters.

Session 11

Regulatory and Legal Aspects

1. Review of the International Banking Act
2. Examination and regulation of asset portfolios
3. Regulation of Euromarkets
4. The regulatory environment in selected countries
5. Legal aspects of international loan agreements

Readings: Donaldson, Chapter 7; D.L. Allen and I.H. Giddy, "Competition and
Cooperation in International Banking Regulation" (xeroxed).

Session 12   Monday, 27 April 1981

Competing for Multinational Corporate Clients

1. MNC funding requirements
2. Factors affecting MNC banking behavior
3. Services to MNCs
4. Organizing for MNC management

Readings: Davis, Chapters 8-10

Session 13   Monday, 4 May 1981

Structuring an International Bank

1. Evaluating competitive strengths and weaknesses
2. Georgraphic vs. industry design
3. Profit attribution and evaluation
4. Resource management and allocation
5. Assessment of effectiveness

Readings: R.E. Radez, "Applying Industry Specialization Internationally"
(xeroxed).

Case: First National City Bank: Multinational Corporate Banking (A),(B),(C),(D).
ICCH 4-476-082/079/080/082.

Session 14   Monday, 11 May 1981

International Banking Strategy

1. Assessment of internal resources
2. Evolution of principle markets
3. Competitive evaluation of strengths and weaknesses
4. Market positioning
5. Management philosophy

Discussion: Group reports

Final Examination   Friday,29 May 1981

Announces the publication of innovative educational materials in Business Administration, Economics and Political Science from leading scholars and universities.

Business Administration Reading Lists & Course Outlines
A new series of 14 volumes ranging from traditional subjects such as *Finance* and *Accounting* to less conventional ones such as *Business, Government & Society* and *Health Administration.*

Political Science Reading Lists & Course Outlines
Another new series whose 11 volumes range from *Political Theory* to *International Relations* and *Public Policy.* It includes the reading lists for Yale Ph.D. exams in 14 fields.

Economics Reading Lists, Course Outlines, Exams, Puzzles & Problems
This 25 volume series updates the original series compiled in July 1980, with the addition of exams, puzzles & problems, including preliminary examinations for graduate students in 16 fields at the Universities of Chicago, Michigan and Washington.

These paper bound volumes cover a sampling of both undergraduate and graduate courses at 72 major colleges and universities. They are designed to widen the horizons of individual professors and curriculum committees and to expand the possibilities for independent study and re-search. Some include suggestions for term paper topics, and many of the lists are useful guides for students seeking both topics and references for term papers and theses. They should enable faculty members to advise students more effectively and efficiently. They will also be useful to prospective graduate students seeking more detailed information about various graduate programs; to those currently preparing for field examinations; and to librarians responsible for acquisitions. Finally, they will be of interest to researchers and administrators who wish to know more about how their own work and the work of their depart-ment is being received by the profession.
The Economics exams, puzzles & problems include both undergraduate and graduate exams. They will be useful to professors in making up exams and problem sets, and to students studying for comprehensive exams.

Libraries and departments may wish to order entire collections, while individual professors and students may wish to purchase volumes in specific areas of interest.

All volumes have ISBN numbers and are listed in the Library of Congress catalog.

A partial list of Universities represented:

University of California, Berkeley
University of California, Los Angeles
University of California at Los Angeles
University of Chicago
Columbia University
Cornell University
Dartmouth College
Duke University
Harvard University
University of Illinois
Indiana University
Johns Hopkins University
London School of Economics & Political Science

Massachusetts Institute of Technology
University of Michigan
University of Minnesota
Northwestern University
University of Pennsylvania
Princeton University
University of Rochester
Stanford University
University of Toronto
University of Washington
University of Western Ontario
University of Wisconsin
Yale University

Political Science Reading Lists and Course Outlines

Compiled by Allan Kornberg, *Duke University*

Volume 1 — **Political Philosophy and Theory** including distributive justice and history of political theory, 224 pages.

Volume 2 — **Conduct of Political Inquiry** including formal logics and political arguments, research technique, theory construction, quantitative methods, and biological, sociological & psychological approaches to politics, 249 pages.

Volume 3 — **American Politics I:** the American congress, the presidency, and the American political system, 229 pages.

Volume 4 — **American Politics II:** American Political Parties, State Local & Urban Politics, Constitutional Law & Judicial Process, 268 pages.

Volume 5 — **Theories of International Relations** including science & technology in international affairs, current issues, nationalism & imperialism, 169 pages.

Volume 6 — **Foreign Policy, International Law, and the Politics of International Security** including Soviet and American foreign policy, defense policy, arms control, and evaluating nuclear strategy, 216 pages.

Volume 7 — **Comparative Politics** including comparative communism & totalitarianism, political participation & electoral behavior, and politics of ethnicity, immigration & cultural pluralism, 237 pages.

Volume 8 — **Area Studies in Comparative Politics** including Africa, Western Europe, Latin America, Canada, China and Japan, 224 pages.

Volume 9 — **Political Economy** including the politics of regulation and international political economy, 191 pages.

Volume 10 — **Political Economy of Development** including political development, problems of transitional societies, multinational corporations and underdevelopment, 165 pages.

Volume 11 — **Public Policy and Policy Analysis** including politics of the environment and media, 272 pages.

Business Administration Reading Lists and Course Outlines

Compiled by James W. Dean, *Columbia University* & *Simon Fraser University* and Richard Schwindt, *Simon Fraser University*.

Volume 1 — **Finance I** — Financial Theory, Financial Institutions and Money Markets, 131 pages.

Volume 2 — **Finance II** — Corporate Finance & Investments, 172 pages.

Volume 3 — **International Banking & Finance**, 145 pages.

Volume 4 — **International Business**, 130 pages.

Volume 5 — **Industrial Relations**, 163 pages.

Volume 6 — **Accounting I** — Financial & Managerial Accounting, 172 pages.

Volume 7 — **Accounting II** — Theory, Auditing, Taxation, History, Accounting for the Non-profit Organization & Multinational Firm, & Accounting Communication, 194 pages.

Volume 8 — **Marketing I** — Marketing Theory, Research, Management & Strategy, 192 pages.

Volume 9 — **Marketing II** — Product, Price, Place & Promotion, 221 pages.

Volume 10 — **Organizational Behavior**, 240 pages.

Volume 11 — **Quantitative Methods & Computer Applications in Business**, 161 pages.

Volume 12 — **Business Policy & Strategy**, 153 pages.

Volume 13 — **Business, Government & Society**, 134 pages.

Volume 14 — **Health Administration**, 315 pages.

Publication date: October 1981. 30% discount on multiple copies of the same volume for classroom use. Orders by individuals must be accompanied by payment. Institutions may request billing. Full refund if returned within 30 day examination period. Payment accepted in U.S. funds only. Outside North America add 10% for additional postage and handling.

Eno River Press
Box 4900, Duke Station
Durham, N.C. 27706
USA

Political Science

☐ Vol. 1	$13	☐ Vol. 7	$13
☐ Vol. 2	$13	☐ Vol. 8	$12
☐ Vol. 3	$13	☐ Vol. 9	$12
☐ Vol. 4	$14	☐ Vol. 10	$12
☐ Vol. 5	$12	☐ Vol. 11	$14
☐ Vol. 6	$13	☐ Complete Set $135	

Business Administration

☐ Vol. 1	$12	☐ Vol. 7	$12	☐ Vol. 13	$10
☐ Vol. 2	$13	☐ Vol. 8	$14	☐ Vol. 14	$15
☐ Vol. 3	$12	☐ Vol. 9	$14	☐ Complete Set $155	
☐ Vol. 4	$11	☐ Vol. 10	$14		
☐ Vol. 5	$13	☐ Vol. 11	$12		
☐ Vol. 6	$13	☐ Vol. 12	$10		

Economics Reading Lists, Course Outlines, Exams, Puzzles & Problems

Compiled by Edward Tower, *Duke University*

Volume 1 — **Microeconomics Course Materials** including oligopoly & game theory, theory of information, social insurance and the economics of technological change, 288 pages.

Volume 2 — **Microeconomics Exams, Puzzles & Problems** including the University of Chicago Ph.D. core exams in price theory 1967 - 1981, 290 pages.

Volume 3 — **Macroeconomics, Monetary Economics and Money & Banking Course Materials**, 301 pages.

Volume 4 — **Macroeconomics, Monetary Economics and Money & Banking Exams, Puzzles & Problems** including the University of Chicago M.A. comprehensive exams in micro and macroeconomic theory, Ph.D. core exams in the theory of income, and M.A. & Ph.D. preliminary exams in money and banking 1967 - 1981, 336 pages.

Volume 5 — **Development Economics Course Materials**, 208 pages.

Volume 6 — **Development Economics Exams, Puzzles & Problems**, 134 pages.

Volume 7 — **Industrial Organization & Regulation Course Materials**, 204 pages.

Volume 8 — **Industrial Organization & Regulation Exams, Puzzles & Problems**, 143 pages.

Volume 9 — **International Economics Course Materials**, 239 pages.

Volume 10 — **International Economics Exams, Puzzles & Problems**, 210 pages.

Volume 11 — **Public Finance Course Materials**, 211 pages.

Volume 12 — **Public Finance Exams, Puzzles & Problems**, 209 pages.

Volume 13 — **Comparative Economic Systems Course Materials** including economic anthropology, economic planning and the economics of socialism, 179 pages.

Volume 14 — **Comparative Economic System Exams, Puzzles & Problems, & the hit para economics articles,** Ed Leamer's list of the m frequently cited economics articles 1895- 197 160 pages.

Volume 15 — **Labor Economics Course Mater** including economics of education and economic demographic interrelations, 208 pages.

Volume 16 — **Labor Economics Exams, Puzzl Problems**, including economic demography, 1

Volume 17 — **Econometrics Course Materials** including macro-econometric modelling, forecas simulation, 175 pages.

Volume 18 — **Econometrics Exams, Puzzles Problems**, 237 pages.

Volume 19 — **Mathematical Economics and Mathematical Models of Economic Growth, 1** pages.

Volume 20 — **Public Choice, Political Econom and the Economics of Public Policy & Law** including radical & utopian economics, econom models of the political process, income distribut altruism & corruption, social choice & game the the economics of war, race and justice, 208 pa

Volume 21 — **Economics of the Environmen Natural Resources and Energy** including fish economics and the economics of Middle East 238 pages.

Volume 22 — **Agricultural Economics**, 222 pa

Volume 23 — **Economic History** 249 pages.

Volume 24 — **History of Economic Thought**, pages.

Volume 25 — **Urban and Regional Economic** pages.

Volumes 1, 3, 5, 7, 9, 11, 13, 15 and 17 contain reading lists & course outlines with exams & pr sets keyed to them. The even-numbered volu between 2 and 18 consist of exams, puzzles problems which are unrelated to the material odd-numbered volumes. Finally, volumes 19 contain all three types of material. 12% of the material in this collection is reprinted from the compilation.

Economics

☐ Vol. 1	$14	☐ Vol. 7	$12	☐ Vol. 14	$10	☐ Vol. 21	$13
☐ Vol. 2	$14	☐ Vol. 8	$11	☐ Vol. 15	$12	☐ Vol. 22	$12
☐ Vol. 3	$14	☐ Vol. 9	$13	☐ Vol. 16	$11	☐ Vol. 23	$13
☐ Vol. 4	$15	☐ Vol. 10	$13	☐ Vol. 17	$12	☐ Vol. 24	$12
☐ Vol. 5	$13	☐ Vol. 11	$13	☐ Vol. 18	$12	☐ Vol. 25	$12
☐ Vol. 6	$11	☐ Vol. 12	$13	☐ Vol. 19	$11	☐ Complete Set $275	
		☐ Vol. 13	$12	☐ Vol. 20	$12		